GH00703056

African Encounters

A memoir by John R Pritchard

Editing and layout by Jenny Knowles

First published in December 2015
Publisher - Little Knoll Press

ISBN No. 978-0-9927220-8-1

Copies of this book can be obtained from
the author
www.LittleKnollBookshop.co.uk
and from bookshops by request.

Printed in Great Britain by
Hobbs the Printers
Totton, Hampshire

For Daniel, Bethany and Nicola

CHAPTER INDEX

Preface

I remember, at primary school, staring every day at the map of the world. Large expanses were coloured pink; others, but not so many, were green. I thought, naively, how good it was to be British, with so much of the world at our feet. Africa, in particular, was almost wholly colonized. Only Liberia, Ethiopia (the map called it Abyssinia), Egypt and South Africa were self-governing and Sudan (an enormous land including the modern South Sudan) was something called an Anglo-Egyptian condominium. The rest of the continent was colonized, mostly by Britain and France, as well as Belgian, Spanish and Portuguese territories.

As the years went by some of my naivety evaporated. I learned about independence movements and freedom fighters. In my first year at university the shocking news of the Sharpeville massacre in Transvaal brought apartheid sharply into my focus, and I took heed of the call for a consumer boycott of South African produce. Africa loomed large in my mind.

I went on to train for ordained ministry in the Methodist Church. My life as a Methodist minister did not turn out as I imagined it would at the outset. It has been my privilege to travel far and wide on church business: from China to Chile, and from Fiji to Finland. I have preached the gospel on six continents, but Africa is the continent with which I have had most to do, living in the Ivory Coast for nine years and later serving as the Africa Secretary of the Methodist Church.

Pat and I were posted to Africa by the Methodist Missionary Society. By the time we came home, and throughout the period when I was on its headquarters staff (1986-1996), the Society was commonly known as the Methodist Church Overseas Division, and usually by the acronym MCOD. Where in these pages I have referred either to 'the Society' or to 'the Division', they are one and the same.

Readers unfamiliar with Methodist structures and terminology should know that in Britain and in most of the Churches established by British Methodists around the world, local churches are grouped together in circuits; that circuits are grouped into Districts and the governing body of the Church is called 'the Conference'. In some countries the British tradition, which has a Chair (historically Chairman) of the District and a President of the Conference, is replicated; in others, these leaders are now styled 'Bishops', 'Presiding Bishops' or such like. When an Overseas District of the British Conference (as Methodism in the Ivory Coast was throughout the time we were there) became a self-governing Church in its own right, it was described as becoming an 'autonomous Conference' – the word 'independent' was properly shunned on the grounds that as partner Churches we are inter-dependent and that we are all dependent on God's grace.

In these memoirs I have reported only occasionally on the content of meetings, discussions and consultations in which I took part, since for the most part they concerned issues which, however significant at the time for those engaged in debating them, are no longer of interest to any but church historians. I have referred by name to very few of the individuals I met. Some of them made a great impression on me and yet their names would mean little to most readers. There is for example a footnote in my history of *Methodists and their Missionary Societies 1900-1996*, which mentions Stanley Mogoba, Itumeleng Mosala and Mvume Dandala, who became good friends. We met from time to time both in South Africa and in England. Only Stanley is mentioned, briefly, in these pages. Yet they were prominent not only in the Church but in South Africa's public life. The footnote reads; 'Mogoba became President of the PAC (Pan Africanist Congress), Mosala President of AZAPO (Azanian People's Organization) and Dandala was the COPE (Congress of the People) candidate in the Republic's 2009 presidential election.'

These pages however, are reminiscences of my personal life and journeys, most of which had no place in official reports I wrote, but which have stayed with me long after the event. My memory has been refreshed by reading letters I wrote home to my parents from the Ivory Coast. I am grateful that they kept them; I wish more had survived.

Some of the countries I visited have changed their names since I was there. The Ivory Coast itself is now officially known, even in English, as Côte d'Ivoire, because its government grew tired of having to shunt from I to C at international meetings, depending on the language according to which seating was arranged! Upper Volta became Burkina Faso and Dahomey became the Republic of Bénin, while the Democratic Republic of Congo was known, at the time of my visits, as Zaïre.

CHAPTER 1

How it all Began

I first became aware of the world church when I arrived in Bristol as an 18 year old undergraduate in 1959. I had in my schooldays been a JMA collector: the quaintly-named Juvenile Missionary Association raised funds for the Methodist Missionary Society, and I had a collecting book and a list of subscribers on whom I would call regularly for their contributions. I had read the literature. I must have heard missionary sermons. I had received books about David Livingstone and John Williams as Sunday School prizes. But in Bristol the second-hand was transformed when I joined the Methodist Society and was assigned to David Phiri's MethSoc group.

David was the first African I got to know; as far as I recall he was the first black person I had ever met. I had been at a multicultural – or, at any rate, a bicultural – school: at Manchester Grammar School there was a separate Jewish assembly every morning. But in class we were not conscious of our differences, and learned little about them. My Jewish class-mates studied the Greek text of Mark, chapters 1–6, in what was called Religious Education on the timetable but was in effect an extra Greek class. It was not a cross-cultural encounter.

David Phiri came from Northern Rhodesia, still a British colony; Zambia became independent only in 1964 and he was one of the earliest cohorts of Zambian graduates. I did not know this when, in Freshers' Week, I arrived at the University Golf Club stand where I'd been told I would find him. Innocently, I asked the British student, "Are you David Phiri?" and got the deadpan reply, "No, he'll be here this afternoon."

David became captain of the Golf Club and later got an Oxford golf blue; later still he became big in Zambian Consolidated Copper Mines, Chairman of the Zambian Football Association and enjoyed the occasional round of golf with President Kenneth Kaunda. Yet he had never played golf before arriving in Bristol.

In those pre-independence days he had earned pocket money by caddying, but only white Rhodesians could play.

David was a genial and devout friend. University was an exciting time; I represented Bristol in debating tournaments, failed to make the cross-country team, became President of MethSoc, was elected to the Students' Union Council and was a Bristol rep to the National Union of Students. David's friendship influenced my plans for the future. Although Zambia was not yet independent, the decolonization of Africa was well under way. The 1960s were designated the UN Decade of Development which we all believed was going to do for the less developed world what the Marshall Plan did for post-war Europe. The East-West cold war might persist, but the North-South wealth gap would be bridged. In those days there was a scheme whereby some people did their post-graduate education year at Makerere in Uganda, coupled with a two-year teaching appointment in East Africa. Some of my friends did it, and I had the same idea.

But my plans changed; perhaps I should say, God had other plans. I went on to Wesley House in Cambridge and read theology. But I still had the urge to work in Africa, while I was in the prime of life. Each year an Officer of the Missionary Society would visit the College and interview the students. In my first year it was Douglas Thompson, General Secretary of the MMS, previously a China missionary who knew about my family (my great-aunt Nell Pritchard had worked in Hubei from 1914 to 1938, while my young cousins the Cundalls and their parents were in Nigeria in the 1950s). He had no difficulty in persuading me to volunteer.

There was however a complication. I was by now engaged, and Pat had just been diagnosed with diabetes. We sought medical advice. One consultant was adamant: it was an absurd idea, the risks were much too great, we should abandon the project. Another told us not to let diabetes rule our lives, Pat too was in her prime, there was no reason not to pursue it. We went ahead – and learned not long afterwards that Archbishop Trevor Huddleston (at the time Bishop of Masasi in Tanzania) had been living with diabetes for ten years.

We were asked where we hoped to be deployed. I did not know then how many people, in the history of MMS, had given their answer and then been sent somewhere else! We opted for West Africa, on the grounds that home leave (furlough) would be taken every two years. In other parts of the world, where the climate was less rigorous or where, as in India, there were hill stations where you could escape the punishing heat for a few weeks' local leave each year, furlough came less often. We needed a thorough diabetic check-up back in Britain at a reasonably frequent interval – and it would be good to see our parents too!

West Africa it was. We imagined we'd be sent to Nigeria, where there was a much bigger missionary contingent than anywhere else on the west coast. This was exciting; church union negotiations were well advanced in Nigeria, as they seemed to be in England, and I shared in the widespread hope that denominational labels would be shed as Anglicans, Methodists and others merged their identity. It did not happen in England or Nigeria. And we were posted to the Ivory Coast.

The Ivory Coast – Côte d'Ivoire – was a French colony until it became independent in 1960. In those days its population was around five or six million, speaking between them 77 different Ivoirian tongues, not counting the languages of migrants from neighbouring countries.

French was the official language, and we were sent to Paris to 'brush up our French' and 'assimilate the French culture'. Eight weeks after leaving Cambridge and six after getting married, we arrived at the Gare du Nord and took a taxi to the 8th arondissement to begin a seven months' extended honeymoon. It was the first time we had used a passport. We went to daily classes at the Alliance Française and I also attended some courses at the Paris Missionary Society's Ecole des Missions. I don't remember what they were; for most of the time I was struggling to follow the French. My preparation for cross-cultural encounter would be done in Africa, primarily through trial and many errors.

One of the earliest errors occurred in Paris. We met on the Place Saint Augustin, a young Ghanaian woman whom we knew;

she lived in the student foyer above the English-speaking Methodist Church on Rue Roquépine. We conversed briefly, and I complimented her on the exquisite black stockings she was wearing. After we parted, Pat said to me, "I think they were probably her legs."

I decided to grow a beard. Six days in, I had a phone call from Erris Tribbeck, the minister at Rue Roquépine. He'd taken a break in Jersey and bad weather had delayed his return – would I kindly conduct the Harvest Festival service the following morning? I agreed but declined to shave; I began by saying, "I stand before you as an illustration of how God makes all things grow."

But we were not supposed to get too involved in the Anglophone community. Assimilating the French culture meant strolling along the banks of the Seine after class, having a sandwich lunch in the Jardins du Luxembourg, visiting museums, going (on the few occasions we could afford it) to the Opera Comique or the Comédie Française. The extended honeymoon was a bonus except in one respect: our digs consisted of one room with single beds, toe to toe, along one wall.

French had not been my favourite subject at school; I was a classicist. Oral French I had never used until we arrived in Paris. But, ten years after I'd dropped school French, I contrived to pass my Diplôme de Français Parlé et Ecrit. It was time to be on our way to Africa.

CHAPTER 2

First encounters

By the mid-1960s, air travel was becoming more common, but we sailed from Amsterdam on the MV *Angolakust*. We were allowed to take more baggage on the initial voyage than an airline would carry. A firm called 'Allisons' supplied various requirements including a couple of camp beds complete with mosquito nets, a strong box and a cash box, which are still in use almost fifty years later – apart from the nets, long since perished. I took a shelf-full of indispensable books; some of them are still on my shelves, with the smell of Africa on them.

The ship was 24 hours late sailing, which gave us the chance to take a train to the Keukenhof gardens (then a fraction of their present size) and see the tulips in their early May glory.

On embarking, we found we were the only passengers and would eat at the Captain's table – but after enjoying one meal, we were confined to our cabin by an almighty storm in the English Channel and all thought of eating was banished. To keep her diabetes stable, Pat consumed practically all the glucose we had with us for the first few months ashore. At our first port of call, Bordeaux, we headed for a pharmacy to restock: an unsteady walk as we recovered our land-legs.

Then came the Bay of Biscay, a millpond by comparison, and on to Dakar, accompanied by schools of dolphins and shoals of flying fish. It had taken a fortnight to reach Africa.

Dakar was a pleasant climate, but anchored off Freetown we got our first taste of tropical humidity. The *Angolakust* was not air-conditioned; we began to learn that we could not expect to get our skin dry.

That night we rode out a storm in Fourah Bay, watching the lightning play behind the Lion Mountains until, when the rain arrived, I could pace the deck in my swimming trunks to cool down. "Mad Englishman," commented the Captain.

Here the ship took on another 20 crew, half whom were quartered on the deck, for the next few legs of the voyage.

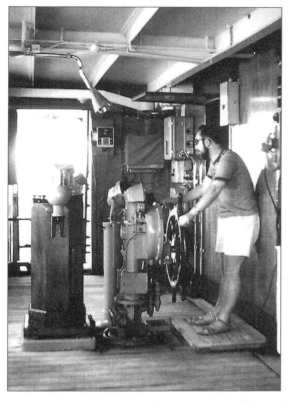

One day we were invited onto the bridge and even took the wheel. What a straight wake we left behind us, until the Captain revealed that we were on auto-pilot. What a sinuous wake when he briefly switched it off!

One morning we awoke to find land to port, a coastline of shimmering palm trees. By late afternoon we were steaming up the Vridi canal into the lagoon to anchor in the harbour, soaking up the views of Abidjan which, in those days, was the political as well as the commercial capital of Ivory Coast. When we docked at the quay, Avril Firman came to greet us. She was secretary to the Chairman of the Methodist District. We disembarked next morning; she saw us through all the formalities and drove us to the flat which would be our home for a few weeks until we moved upcountry to my first post. She informed us that we were invited to the evening meal at the Chairman's house on the Plateau (the city centre) and that he would send his chauffeur to pick us up.

The car duly arrived and we took the back seat. We drove across the one and only bridge over the lagoon to the Plateau, and pulled up outside the District offices. The Chairman lived upstairs. It was only when we'd been shown in that it dawned on us that our driver was in fact the Chairman himself!

Samson Nandjui was the first African to lead the Ivoirian Church. Methodism in Côte d'Ivoire was built on the foundations of a brief but amazingly fruitful evangelistic mission conducted by the Liberian, William Wadé Harris, between mid-1913 and early 1915. The converts had been brought under Methodist care in the course of the 1920s and 1930s; the first Ivoirian ministers were ordained in 1939; Nandjui had taken office at the Harris Jubilee of 1964 amid great jubilation.

We had some interesting conversations in the course of the first few months as I struggled with my French. On one occasion he apparently asked me if Pat was pregnant. I mistook his question and responded nonchalantly, "Oui, oui" – which was not the case at all. He clarified the matter some weeks later; his wife Sabine had looked Pat over and assured him no offspring was on the way.

One of the first questions I asked, concerned the town of Divo, where we were to live, and what my responsibilities would be.

With Solomon Attangba, after John's ordination.

The answer was simple: Visit the churches. How many? I gathered it was a lot. The circuit was under the care of the Chairman; there was one colleague, Salomon Attangba, who had just been ordained and lived twenty miles away. His sector contained almost a hundred chapels, mine a mere sixty.

In the weeks before we moved there, we were befriended by two European couples, whose friendship has proved as durable as the camp beds. Our flat was one of two above the Youth Centre in the Treichville quarter of the city, and next door lived Jean-Jacques and Claudine Buard, he a Swiss minister and youth worker, with their adorable adopted infant, Jean-François. They showed us the ropes: took us shopping, introduced us to the bank and helped us set up an account, got us involved in some of the youth activities.

Philip and Judith Chapman lived inland at Agboville, on the country's one railway from Abidjan north to

Jean-François Buard.

Burkina Faso (in those days still called 'Upper Volta'). We went and stayed with them for a few days and Philip took me on trek to visit some of the villages. That weekend was pretty much the extent of my preparation for the work I had come to do; it was invaluable and it was essential. I learned the etiquette of village life.

Philip and I drove in a battered Renault 4, accompanied by a catechist – one of the circuit's lay agents. Each circuit in the District had a number of these, some housed and paid a pittance, some on a voluntary basis. Each catechist cared for one, or maybe up to a dozen, of the village churches. They were local people who spoke the language. Given the multiplicity of Ivoirian languages, it was quite likely that an African minister would find himself as dependent on them as a European. Our trek that weekend involved two native tongues; one of them, Krobou, is spoken in only three villages in the world.

We bumped along corrugated laterite roads and rough lanes until, on the outskirts of the first, we were greeted by a crowd of singing, ululating villagers. Philip's arrival had been announced. We were escorted into the village and climbed out of the car.

A ritualised exchange of greetings ensued, conducted in bush French; I give the gist of it in English.

"What is the news?" we were asked.

"All is well," replied Philip. "We have been looking forward to coming today and we have arrived. The journey was good. What is your news?"

"We heard you were coming today and we have been waiting for you ever since…" (Early morning is implied, though who knows?) "We waited until we were tired. But you are here."

Village welcome.

The etiquette then required a visit to the village headman to greet him. Afterwards we were shown where we would spend the night, and the camp bed got its first airing.

A room had been vacated for us in one of the more prepossessing houses. In most villages, back then, that meant a mud hut with a thatched roof. Occasionally, in the months to come, I was shown to a posh house: a mud hut with a corrugated iron roof. There was no ceiling, and such a room was intolerably hot. I much preferred the thatch, as long as it was not leaking in the rainy season. At some point, we were told about the programme prepared for our stay in the village. We were served a meal, and left to eat it on our own, though at many a meal children would be gaping at the door and windows.

That weekend we visited four villages, overnighting in two. Philip conducted Saturday evening prayers and 6 am morning prayers; we then drove to a nearby village and held prayers in one of the houses, before returning for a communion service at 9.30. On Sunday afternoon we moved on, and after the customary etiquette, we examined, via the interpreter, candidates for adult baptism and for full church membership. There was an evening service of baptism – twelve infants and five adults – and on the Monday at 6.30 am a communion service at which five new members were received. This church had a brass band which led us back to our lodging after both services, accompanied by the whole congregation. Then on to the last village for morning prayer with baptism and communion.

We returned to Agboville laden with gifts of five hens, six pineapples and six eggs. In the Divo circuit too I would find the generosity of the village churches quite overwhelming, running even to sheep, goats and black hairy pigs.

One Friday lunchtime, while we were still at the flat, I had an unannounced visit from the catechist at the Treichville church. They had a problem: the preacher planned for Sunday, a top civil servant, was in America. Could I help out? Well, this was the work I had come to do. I had preached in French just the once before we left Paris. Now I was in at the deep end. Robert Beugré explained that the church seated 500, but the overflow outside in the compound wouldn't be so big as usual, because the rainy season was threatening – just another couple of hundred. And by the way, the minister would be on the front row.

"The minister?" I asked. "Why are you approaching me?"

"Oh, not the pastor – he's just come out of hospital. I mean the Minister of Information."

And there he was, a cabinet minister in my first congregation. It all went just as Robert foretold – though I was taken aback when, the moment I announced my text, the choir burst into song. '*Parle, parle, Seigneur ...*' (Speak, Lord; your servant is listening ...) to a tune written by Samson Nandjui's brother, Abraham, which was, it turned out, often sung at this point in Methodist services.

The deep end was not finished with me. Each Sunday, the national radio broadcast an act of worship, with canned hymns and a reflection. I was scheduled to record the reflection on the Saturday before we went off to Divo. It must have been acceptable, since in the coming years I did it frequently. A few days later, in our brand new but very basic Renault 4, we moved.

The Ivory Coast.

CHAPTER 3

Divo

Our arrival in Divo was more low key than in the villages I had visited with Philip. The choir waited until Sunday to come to the manse door and escort us to the church, singing and dancing. But Pierre Dja, the local catechist, and some of the elders were waiting, vying with each other to show us around. It was a while since they'd had a European minister. The bungalow had running water and electricity, more than we had dared to hope as we left England. It had rats in the roof and cockroaches everywhere, but that was normal. It also came complete with a groundsman (known in those days as a 'yard-boy') and a nightwatchman.

Employing staff was out of our comfort zone; little did I know that one day, in London, I'd have a hundred on the books. However, they knew the ropes and we could leave them to it.

Tassalé, the groundsman, and his wife Pauline, lived in the garden and taught us much, especially not to let the grass grow longer than an inch in case a snake was hiding behind a blade.

Pauline prepares foutou.

A dozen different tropical fruits grew in the garden. In case they did not suffice, two different well-wishers each brought us a stem of bananas laden with bunches; we hung them one at either end of the veranda and promised ourselves to eat one every time we passed.

After a few weeks someone asked us, *"Etes-vous climatisés?"* I forget who asked; it may have been one of the Italian priests, or perhaps one of the Lebanese shopkeepers. In many a small town all over west Africa, enterprising Lebanese or Syrian émigrés kept a general store. By that time we had begun to be acclimatised. There came the morning when I said, "It's a bit chilly today," checked the thermometer and saw that it was 80° (we English always used the Fahrenheit scale in those days). But the enquiry meant something different: *Have you got an air-conditioner?* For us, that was a luxury too far.

210 km northwest of Abidjan, Divo town had a population of around 5,000 in 1966. It is in the heart of Dida country, where it is vital to know the words *Ayoka* (hello) and *Ayunkwa* (thank you). Still needing to improve my French, I learned few other Dida words in the eleven months we spent there; although, from hearing them used frequently by interpreters, I was soon able to say 'Let us sing a hymn', 'Let us pray' and 'Please sit down' for myself. There were also Baoulé villages in the neighbourhood (the Baoulé were the largest tribe in the country) and some Wobé encampments.

A Dida village.

Divo was reached by a tarred road from Abidjan, which continued to Lakota and beyond. All other roads in the area were red laterite or rutted tracks, dusty or muddy depending on the season. Most of the villages where there were Methodist chapels, were marked on no map. I made a map as time went by. Some villages were a sixty mile drive away, and one was much further to get to if you didn't want to risk wading across a river where crocodiles lurked.

It was part virgin rainforest and partly cultivated bush. On the drive from Abidjan, you passed a large commercial pineapple plantation. These days you would also pass vast oil palm plantations, where the deforestation has destroyed the jungle. The villagers grew sweet bananas, plantains, yams, coffee and cocoa, along with subsistence crops on their gardens and allotments. They were mostly self-employed, which meant that any day of the week when the minister showed up they could down tools and do Sunday-type activities. The sun set between 6 pm and 7 pm all year round, and there was no electricity in the villages, so choir practice, even three times a week, was well attended. The Dida were a musical people. On our

The choir processes to Divo church.

first Sunday in Divo the choir sang Handel's Hallelujah Chorus unaccompanied – as fine a rendition as I've heard anywhere except, perhaps, in Fijian in Suva. Some of the choirmasters were amazing. One of them needed to listen to a single verse of an unknown hymn and could then teach all four lines of the harmony to his choir.

Cash income for most rural households arrived in quantity only once a year at harvest-time, when the trucks of coffee- and cocoa-buyers braved (or created) the quagmires that rendered many of the routes virtually impassable. With the proceeds, school fees were paid, new clothes bought and, after a good harvest, progress might be made in improving the house. In most villages and at sites dotted along the main roads, half-built brick buildings, covered in undergrowth, were to be seen. The greenery would be removed and a few more layers of brick added after the next harvest. Brick churches were built in the same way: the Harvest Festival was the year's major fundraiser. Great rejoicing always attended the day when the roof was added, although there was still much to do before the building was complete.

Divo town itself had a thriving market and a handful of shops, a poorly-staffed hospital with a maternity ward that averaged a hundred live births every week, a Roman Catholic church with two Italian priests, and several schools. We lived on a compound with the church next door and a Methodist primary school behind.

When term began, two months after we arrived, life became much noisier. The nearest classroom to our veranda housed 'Year One', children starting school at the age of six or seven. That year they came from homes where, between them, sixteen different tongues were spoken, and they had to begin by learning French in order to be taught in French. Periodically through the day, we would hear the chant *Je me lève, je m'assois, j'ouvre la porte* etc.

When I preached in the town church, my sermon was translated, sentence by sentence, first into Dida and then into Baoulé. This gave me the chance to ponder my next sentence carefully, although to the hearer it was terribly disjointed and even more conducive to letting the mind wander than most sermons are.

My working pattern involved conducting a communion service in Divo on the first Sunday of the month, probably with a run out to one of the nearer churches for an afternoon service. The other weekends saw me on trek, away for one or two nights. At first Pat came with me, and was treated as if no white woman had ever been in the village – which was almost certainly the case. But the unpredictability of meal times times upset her diabetes, and she soon opted to remain at home. She got used to my returning with bountiful gifts, but the hairy black swine were a challenge. Our domestic staff were Muslims and wouldn't touch them, and her home economics lessons had never taught her to slaughter pigs.

In between the treks, weekdays were occupied with keeping the circuit accounts (double-entry book-keeping, which I also learnt in situ with Avril Firman's help), the time-consuming task of preparing sermons in French, or receiving unannounced visitors. The school head or a teacher might drop in, or a catechist from an outlying area who'd come into town to market, or some of the educated women who could talk to Pat: the sound of a hand-clap and the call '*ko-ko-ko*', announcing their presence, punctuated the day. I did some home visits in the town, but the urgent task was to visit all the churches.

Pierre and Gabriel, two of the circuit catechists.

It was the custom, inherited from early missionaries, to sign the membership booklets of every communicant. On one occasion I observed that a woman had not been to communion for four years. I enquired why: had she been disciplined, excommunicated for some reason? Had she been ill? No, I was told. This was her first opportunity. The others had evidently attended services elsewhere, but this was the first time in four years that this village had seen a minister. My African predecessor had no car. He had to rely on infrequent and unpredictable public transport, a sort of minibus with a super-charged roof-rack known as a *mille-kilos*, to get around. He spent a lot of time waiting at the roadside to move on, or to get home. With the car, doing three treks a month, it took me nine months to visit them all. I baptized over 500 adults and considerably more babies and children.

In the space of ten months, the *ko-ko-ko* at the door brought messengers from a total of ten villages to say, 'Pastor, we've built a church in our village; will you come and hold a service?' For one reason or another, a group of Methodists found themselves in a village with no church, and even if the nearest church was only a kilometre or two away, they wanted a church in their own village. With their own hands and traditional techniques, they had put up a pole-and-dagga hut, thatched with woven palm or banana leaves. They told me how to find the place, and I added it to my map. And when I went, it was not only the small group who turned out; the whole village wanted to know what it was that mattered so much they'd gone to the trouble of building a hut they weren't going to live in. Oversight had to be assigned to one of the catechists, who would arrange for preachers from neighbouring churches to meet with them, ideally Sunday by Sunday, but probably less often.

Thus the sixty churches entrusted to my care became seventy within a year. The Church in the Ivory Coast – not just around Divo – was growing apace.

Preachers were, by and large, devout men. Some of them were leaders in the civil life of the village. I do not recall any women preachers, though many women served devotedly as class-leaders (Methodist readers will understand the term). But many of the preachers were illiterate. They could not read the Bible for themselves, although the gospels had been translated into Dida in the 1920s. They relied on the Bible stories they had heard from others. Catechists were encouraged to meet with the preachers in their section on Fridays and go over the week's Bible readings with them, and hopefully give them the outline of a sermon – I did this when I was able to attend such meetings. The preacher would make his way home rehearsing the sermon to himself and putting its message into his village context. Some walked many miles in each direction, greeting people on the way and 'gossiping the gospel'.

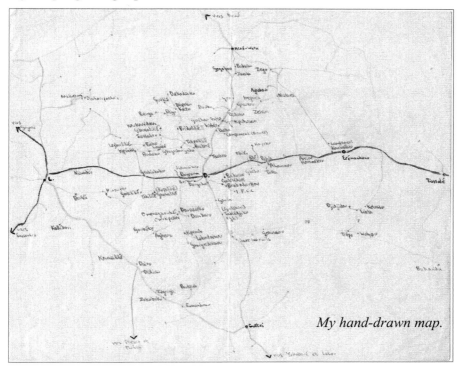

My hand-drawn map.

Four times a year, the circuit held a Quarterly Meeting, following what was then the British pattern. But we held two – one in Salomon Attangba's half of the circuit, with its ninety-odd chapels, and one at the Divo end. Salomon, my senior, presided at both. These meetings lasted three days: on Tuesday evening, the Finance Committee, on Wednesday, the Preachers' Meeting in the morning and the Class-Leaders' Meeting to follow. A gathering of the catechists might well be slotted in as well. On Thursday, a communion service was followed by the full business meeting. In the evening, for some light relief, a choir competition. On Friday there was the Youth Leaders' meeting and then we went home.

Methodists like to begin the New Year with a Covenant Service to renew their Christian commitment. With the help of my team of catechists, we agreed it could be done. We selected seven of the larger villages, with good-sized chapels, and I would drive to four of them on 1st January and another three on the 2nd. The other churches in the vicinity were invited to assemble there. They came, mostly on foot, from early morning, with their choirs and brass bands and food for a feast, and spent the day partying to welcome the New Year. When I arrived, the hubbub stopped, and we gathered in and around the chapel and worshipped. It worked well, and we did the same on Easter Sunday and Monday.

On 2nd January, driving up a steep, winding and narrow road to my seventh service, I met a vehicle coming down too fast and damaged the front of the car. We didn't let it spoil the celebrations, but by the time I was on my way home, night had fallen and I crawled back with no headlights.

Meanwhile, however, someone had gone to Divo and reported to Pat that I'd had an accident.

"What happened?" she asked. "Oh, nothing serious," came the reply, "but he has lost an eye." Pat went pale. The French for headlight was not in his vocabulary. "*L'oeil de la voiture*," he eventually explained.

Domestic life was varied. We were twice brought new-born babies whose mothers had died in childbirth. Both Simeon and Elizabeth slept in a drawer taken from our chest of drawers, until we were able to take them to the Pouponnière in Dabou, a church-run baby home.

We occasionally had students from the secondary school round to visit. Pat made them a jelly (my mother loved to send items unobtainable in Côte d'Ivoire by the customs-free small packet service), which they prodded uncertainly.

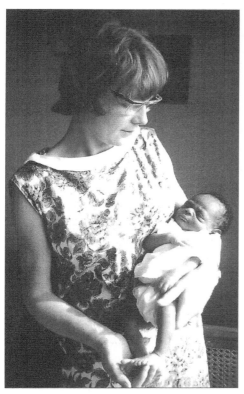
Pat with baby Simeon.

Pauline, our gardener's wife, was pregnant. She had three failed pregnancies behind her. This time she was in labour for 48 hours. Tassalé had to pay for an injection, and we gave him the money, but to no avail. He buried the babe, then, since she had now been four times unlucky, he sent Pauline away. We ourselves were by then in the throes of leaving unexpectedly and lost touch with them both.

CHAPTER 4

A Wedding, a Death and a Departure

There were about twenty Methodist ministers, Ivoirian and European, in the country. So when one got married, we were all invited. Elisée and his bride were wed at Orbaff, an Adjoukrou village. They had been married according to local custom for some time, and their marriage had been registered by civil law. But now Elisée had completed his ministerial training at the Porto Novo seminary in Dahomey (not yet renamed the Republic of Bénin) and was embarking on his ministry. It was time for their union to be blessed in church. I have no idea whether they had taken the decision themselves or whether they were pressurized by the church leadership.

Church weddings were uncommon, for from the beginning the missionaries had recognised the customary rites; their stand against polygamy deterred many, and had they rejected local custom entirely, they and their message would in turn have been rejected outright. It was also the case that any marriage that proved infertile would not survive. Family pressure demanded children. The Catholic priests in Divo made it a categorical rule that they would marry no childless couple, unless a baby was seen to be on the way. Elisée and his bride had no problems there. Their children

were bridesmaids and pageboy. It was not a lavish wedding by European standards, but the clothes and the food were deemed essential to the ceremony and were an expense that most folk would not entertain.

It was good for us to meet colleagues and their spouses in a happy social occasion. The Orbaff church, though not yet fully finished, was a revelation. Why did it have such a very tall tower? Answer: because there was a Roman Catholic church in the village and the Methodists wanted their tower to reach nearer to heaven than the Catholic tower, and since the Methodist site was slightly nearer to sea-level …

Maybe one day these towers would be hung with bells, but at present the summons to worship was issued, as in so many places, by striking a discarded car wheel.

Not long afterwards, in May 1967, I went off to a Quarterly Meeting. On the last morning one of the local preachers, Paul, received a message from his village that his fellow preacher, Amos, who had not come, had died. Paul needed to return at once and make the funeral arrangements. So we said a prayer and he left.

That evening back in Divo, as I was recounting the events to Pat, there was a hand-clap on the veranda and there was Paul. Amos had not died after all, but was seriously ill with tetanus and needed to be brought to the hospital. They'd had him at the roadside that morning waiting for the only *mille-kilos* of the day. Just as it arrived, he appeared to breathe his last, so they put the messenger on the bus instead. But when they got him back to his hut they'd realised Amos had not quite expired. And when Paul returned, on the one *mille-kilos* of the day in the other direction, he'd sized up the situation and gone back to the roadside to thumb a lift. Passing gendarmes had refused to take Amos, but had brought Paul back to Divo. Would I go for Amos?

Most of the way was on a sinuous, rutted, pot-holed track through the jungle and I always avoided such journeys at night, but I could do no other than set out again. Amos was in a bad way; we prayed and then prepared to put him in the car. First, to my consternation, four relatives squeezed in with their food supply, pots and pans and mats – there was no hospital catering and even on the ward they would be the primary carers. Amos was laid across the knees of the three on the back seat and we returned at snail's pace. Every so often a convulsion propelled his feet into the small of my back. We got to the hospital to find that the only doctor was down in the capital for a month on a course, leaving a male nurse in charge. After a long wait, Amos was fixed up on a drip and I went home.

Next day our Swiss friends brought little Jean-François, to stay for a week while they were travelling in the interior, and later I set off for another two nights away. As I left I checked that Amos was hanging on, and on my way home on Monday morning I looked in again, only to find him there no longer. I assumed he'd died, but discovered his family had given up hope and taken him to die in his village. A living man, even if a dying man, is only one fare in a *mille-kilos*; a corpse costs the hire of a car. I understood the economics of their decision, but after the events of Friday night, I was not pleased.

Morning prayers had been early that day. It was only 9.15 am when I reached home. I found Jean-François sitting cheerfully at the breakfast-table but Pat slumped in a chair on the veranda in a diabetic coma. I could not rouse her. I jumped back in the car and sped off to the town's one private doctor, jumped his queue and had him round in no time. He couldn't rouse her either, but offered his fast car, his chauffeur, and his wife, a nurse, to take us into Abidjan. I rang Church headquarters, who arranged for us to take Pat directly to a private clinic, and Jean-François to another friend. I didn't know it, but they asked Frère Jean, a Taizé brother who drove a private ambulance, to come for us. He passed us somewhere on the two and a half hour journey to the capital.

Before we reached Abidjan, Pat came round. The dark thoughts of all the missionary martyrs of bygone days that had kept surfacing, evaporated. Pat had a thorough check for a few days in the clinic; we were given early and extended leave; and when we returned to Côte d'Ivoire in 1968, I was redeployed to Abidjan where there were well-staffed hospitals on the spot. So our time in a country circuit was reduced to just eleven months. It was a formative, transformative period. When I started work in the capital, where most residents were first- or second-generation city-dwellers who would return to their village for the holidays if at all possible, I could relate to their background.

The outcome for us contrasted with the fate of poor Amos, whose memorial service we attended just before we left Divo, and the contrast made a lasting mark. As missionaries, we were among the poorest members of the European community in Côte d'Ivoire, but materially we were rich compared with a Dida coffee-farmer. The divide between rich world and poor world was etched in our experience.

CHAPTER 5

Port Chaplaincy

Our daughter was born in January 1968 in England. I returned to Abidjan in February; Pat and Claire would follow by plane at Easter. Once again I went by sea, this time on a passenger vessel, the *Général Mangin,* from Marseilles. It enabled me to take pushchair, playpen and the rest. The passenger service came to an end a year later, as air travel took over. With time to spare between the night train arrival in Marseilles and embarkation in the afternoon, I visited a barber who removed my beard; I went clean-shaven until it grew as I walked the Pennine Way in the summer of 1984.

I had been away for nine months and the Abidjan skyline had changed: the luxury high-rise Hotel Ivoire across the bay had added a second, taller tower. But I returned to the Treichville apartment for a few weeks. I had been appointed Port and Industrial Chaplain, and in preparation I had spent a term of our furlough at William Temple College in Rugby. While there I had managed to write an article in French, which appeared in *Flambeau,* a quarterly theological review published in Yaoundé. The French was vetted by a Swiss student, Hans Lutz, who was preparing for industrial chaplaincy in Hong Kong – where I caught up with him many years later. Neither of us took responsibility for the misprint which substituted *misère* for *ministère*. Where I had originally written that traditional parish structures were not a suitable 'instrument for ministry in a metropolis', the readership learned that they were not a suitable instrument for misery!

1968 was a good time to take up my new assignment. A new chapel and adjoining house were almost complete in the Cité du Port and they had to be furnished. At that period there was civil war in Nigeria; only much more recently, reading Chimamanda Ngozi Adichie's *Half of a Yellow Sun,* did I come to appreciate just how terrible was the suffering a few hundred miles away along the coast. Côte d'Ivoire was one of a handful of countries that recognised Biafra and was host to large numbers of Biafran refugees, including a group of carpenters who were employed making furniture at the new Methodist Hospital in Dabou, an hour's drive away. Their work there was almost done; they were glad of another contract, and made our table, chairs, sideboard and beds. All was complete and ready to welcome Pat and Claire when they arrived.

La Fraternité du Port.

Abidjan was said to be the fastest growing city in sub-Saharan Africa at the end of the 1960s. (It was probably said of other cities too!) From 1945, Abidjan's population tripled in size every ten years. It was a pole of attraction, not only for the Ivoirian hinterland, but for Mali and Upper Volta as well; Bambara and Moré, the language of the Mossi people, were widely spoken. New industries were constantly recruiting labour. The port itself expanded three-fold over the next seven years.

The Cité du Port comprised an avenue of smart bungalows for the harbourmaster and senior management, who were almost all French, and a 'low income' housing estate for Port Authority employees. Employees of the mercantile companies, warehousemen and dockers, lived elsewhere: many of them newcomers, in squalid shanty-towns at a fair distance. There was a primary school for the children of the estate. Two of the teachers, Daniel and Félix, were the leading lights of the small Protestant congregation. Next to the school was a small mosque, and next to the mosque was the new complex where we lived, named *La Fraternité du Port*.

The Roman Catholic *Chapelle du Port* was at the other side of the estate. I talked with the Catholic chaplains, who belonged to *Les Fils de la Charité,* about how they saw the task. One of them regularly went out to sea with the sardine fishing fleet. To get a feel for it, I went with him on a couple of days.

The fishing port.

The boats were small, the swell was big, my stomach churned and I decided to leave that role to him. Nor did we see much of the seafarers. We might have encountered a few had we loitered with intent at the smart Seaman's Club, but in reality I only went there very rarely, with Pat and the children, to enjoy the pool.

Pat with Claire and Paul relaxing at the Seamen's Club.

Ships spent as little time as possible in harbour, and with the advent of containerisation the turn-round time grew ever shorter.

A quay.

Only if a sailor was brought ashore ill or injured, was there work to be done. I spent a good deal of my time on the quays and in the warehouses, with occasional visits to the Port Authority offices.

The people I met in their workplaces came from many backgrounds. Most had come to Abidjan seeking work, hoping to find the city streets 'paved with gold'. A few were fervent Christians. Some came from Christian homes back in their native village, but away from the social pressure of the family and drawn by the bright lights of the city, had lapsed. The most interesting conversations were with people who knew little of Christianity, and whose village religion centred on the local spirit, associated perhaps with a great tree or a striking rock or a nearby river. It was this spirit or divinity, they believed, who gave or withheld the harvest, the rains, illness and fertility, and who was propitiated by charms, sacrifices and fetishes. But people who had left their village a hundred or more miles away discovered that the spirit had no power in cosmopolitan Abidjan, and a few of them wanted to know more about the God who loved them wherever they were.

I had, to begin with, one colleague. Samuel Traoré was a catechist from Mali with an evangelistic and pastoral ministry among the migrant Bambara-speakers. There were several Bambara congregations, worshipping in classrooms in different quarters of the city. I occasionally visited them, with Samuel to interpret.

I had more direct responsibility for a congregation of migrant Ewé people from eastern Ghana in a coastal village of fishermen and fishwives. When I led worship there, generally once a month, they got out a harmonium and I played as well as preached.

One of their number, Christian Togoh, was the acknowledged and authoritarian leader; he eventually returned to Ghana and became a minister in the African Methodist Episcopal Church Zion, a denomination of American origin.

I was the only English minister in the capital, and I was also asked to take responsibility for the Anglophone congregation which met at the Plateau church once a month. Many of its members worked at embassies or at the African Development Bank or for oil companies. There could be six or seven ambassadors in the pews, British, American, Korean, Liberian, Ghanaian, Zambian, but the majority of the members were Africans. In time the ex-commander of the Biafra navy, in exile with his Trinidadian wife, and the ex-Ghanaian ambassador, who set up an ophthalmological practice when the Busia régime was overthrown, became good friends.

Some of the congregation wanted to meet weekly, but the policy was to encourage people who, after all, used French at work and at the shops to join a local church and share in worship with local people, except for once a month. For my part I could offer no more; I was already at full stretch, but I enjoyed a workload that took me from the dockers to the diplomats.

Our Visitors' Book from those days records numerous guests. Among the first were people who had been sent to represent the British Church at the official opening of the Dabou Hospital. The Methodist Association of Youth Clubs, celebrating its 21st birthday, had raised much of the money to pay for it and provided skilled volunteers who worked with local villagers on the construction, under the supervision of a British engineer.

The opening was performed by the President of the Republic, Félix Houphouet-Boigny. It was a splendid occasion. But that day I had an acute tummy-bug and missed it completely. Of course the hospital had been functioning for a while before the President found a date in his diary. For some years Pat drove to Dabou every Monday to run the X-Ray department, on the basis of a three-day crash course in radiography. Her time as a photographer's apprentice before we married was not wasted: she knew her way around the dark room.

The Renault factory was directly across the road from our house: R4s like mine – assembled from imported components – were produced by the handful every week. The Nestlé factory was more productive. Once, when I was in Ghana, I studied the label on the tin of instant coffee that I was drinking, and the reality of globalisation (a word not yet in vogue) came home to me. Quite possibly the coffee had been grown in Ghana, smuggled into Côte d'Ivoire where the price was higher, processed there by a Swiss company registered, so the tin said, in Nassau and sold back in Ghana. I wondered where the label was printed …

Other industries included sawmills, soap and textile works, a French bakery and two breweries. (They competed not only with their beer, but with their sodas, which were what I was invariably offered in the villages: 'OK Tip Top' and 'Youki-café', a fizzy coffee-flavoured drink, which I preferred to the usual over-sweet orange.) And new factories were opening every month or so. I soon realised that building up industrial chaplaincy on top of what I'd inherited was more than one person could tackle, and I needed a colleague. Emmanuel Yando, who joined the team when he finished his training at the theological college in Porto Novo, was full of enthusiasm and talent – one day he would become the President of the Methodist Church in Côte d'Ivoire.

I was a member of the West Africa Urban-Industrial Committee, set up under the auspices of the All Africa Conference of Churches. It consisted of practitioners from Dakar to Douala and met annually, hosted by one or other of us. I was persuaded to edit its quarterly publication, which appeared in both English and French: *Urban Africa* and *L'Afrique Urbaine*. By this time I was interpreting fairly fluently at bilingual meetings; translating articles and writing editorials was time well spent. It stood me in good stead in years to come.

The first meeting I attended was held in Tema, Ghana, where a young Ghanaian Methodist minister, Joe Bannerman, was appointed as the Tema Christian Council's first Urban Industrial Missioner in 1970. I was not met at Accra Airport and as I had no other directions I took a taxi to Methodist headquarters. It was past nightfall and the offices were closed, but I was welcomed by

Father Grant. Francis Grant entered the ministry in 1915 and was the inaugural President of the Ghana Methodist Church; he was living in retirement on the compound and a very gracious host. I spent the night under his roof and was collected next morning.

Bannerman was a dynamic personality. His new post was funded on a shoestring, and he gave up both the car and the telephone that the Methodist Church provided in order to take it on. He made himself everybody's friend and servant, talking with them at factory gates, in offices, shops and markets, outside the Labour Exchange and inside the Police Station. He said that 'it is not the laity's job to help the minister run the church, it is the minister's job to help the laity change the world'. He was an inspiration to all the committee. I later wrote a foreword to his short book, *The Cry for Justice in Tema*.

Tema was originally a small fishing village. The harbour was built in 1954, shortly before Ghana's independence, to complement the seaport at Takoradi way to the west. Côte d'Ivoire too needed a second seaport and settled on San Pedro, two days' drive to the west of Abidjan.

I first visited San Pedro with the family, driving in our Renault 4 for many miles on a newly cut, as yet untarred, road through the forest, fording some watercourses and ferried across another. We passed a few mud hamlets, but saw almost no-one except the ferryman on the route, until we were stopped by a man with a red flag.

Ferry to San Pedro.

We waited for the boom of an explosion; and then found we had reached the site of the new harbour. The small fishing village still stood, but its occupants had already gone; the civil engineers had their own encampment.

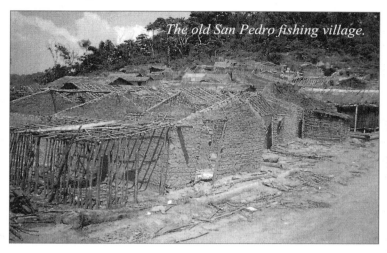

The old San Pedro fishing village.

There was little to see and we set out on the return journey. But within a year or two there was a harbour for eight ships; hills were razed and swamps filled to provide land for houses, factories; and a busy township of 30,000 men, women and children were living there. Methodist migrants were among them from the start, and Philip Chapman became the first minister in San Pedro. Before a multi-purpose hall was built, the thatched shack where they worshipped was moved three times – one Sunday, worship was punctuated by the noise of bulldozers and that afternoon the members sang as they dismantled their chapel and moved on.

Meanwhile, I accumulated other tasks: secretary of the Synod, of the Liturgy Committee, and of the working party that began to prepare for autonomy. It was time for the church to take its government into its own hands, although another decade went by before that was realized. By then we were back in England. We lived at the *Fraternité* for seven years, and left in 1975.

CHAPTER 6

Abidjan Snapshots

The Missionary Society's monthly magazine, *NOW*, produced an issue on *'Living in Cities'* in May 1971. I contributed two vignettes. The first told of my colleague, Samuel ...

'Samuel Traoré came to Abidjan in 1946, when he was about twenty-five years old. His reasons: scratching a living from the soil of Upper Volta was not very exciting; his wife had – temporarily, but not for the last time – 'gone home to mother'; he had heard of the place and was curious.

In the last quarter of a century, hundreds of thousands of Ivorians, Maliens and Voltaics have done the same thing. When Samuel arrived, the population of Abidjan was 44,000; today, it approaches 400,000. The big city is a perpetual temptation to all whose family circumstances allow them any freedom, and to many who simply throw off the natural ties in the pursuit of novelty.

Samuel found work without much trouble: at first as a shopkeeper, then as a laundryman, and for the last few years as a Christian evangelist among his immigrant Bambara compatriots. Today, it is much harder to find employment. Although many new factories are being opened, thousands flock from the country for every hundred new jobs.

Samuel's wife soon joined him. It was not a particularly happy marriage, but they stayed together until 1961 when she returned to Upper Volta for good. In contrast, many marriages not theoretically 'broken' are in fact shattered when a man goes off to Abidjan. The wife, and the children if there are any, stay behind. If he gets a job, he may send money home. But he will live in scandalously confined quarters and only see his family on rare holiday visits. Meanwhile, temporary liaisons are easily formed.

Samuel found a house, too, and he established a relatively simple style of life, before the attractions and distractions of the big city were as great as they are now. All in all, he faced fewer temptations than today's immigrants. With so many people now seeking too few jobs and without a regular income, it is no surprise that there is so much theft. With

Samuel Traoré.

so many people living in discomfort far from the family, it is not astonishing there is so much prostitution. With so much to see and to do, it is small wonder more and more still come to swell the problems.

Samuel's son, who went with his mother in 1961, has just returned to Abidjan. Samuel is worried for his son.

Yet in one respect, today's immigrants are less beset by temptation than was Samuel in 1946. When he came, a Christian, he found no community worshipping in a language he understood well. How easy it would have been to abandon the faith. He recalls how 'If you were a Christian, no Muslim would share his food with you', and that is still largely true. Samuel trod a lonely way, gradually seeking out other Christians among his fellow Bambaras, until today there are three flourishing congregations in the city. The Bambara Christian who arrives in Abidjan today will at once be welcomed into the circle and helped to face temptation, largely thanks to Samuel Traoré.'

A city of 400,000 is not huge by the standards of the early 21st century. But it was then. Demographic statistics are staggering. The global population in 1971 was some 3¾ billion; in 2015 it is almost twice that number. Côte d'Ivoire's population then was 6 million; today it is 24 million. Abidjan's population now approaches 5 million, the sixth largest city in Africa.

Samuel's assessment of Christian-Muslim relations was doubtless justified and probably remains so. But there were exceptions. We got to know some of the regulars at the mosque next door. When Aboubakar got married, we were invited to the ceremony, which was conducted in the crowded, brightly decorated yard of his new in-laws' house. The food was ample and tasty!

The other snapshot was part of a section on *Problems and Temptations of City Life.* I wrote:

> 'Bernadette was brought up in Abidjan, but it was largely a rural upbringing. Her father learned to drive in the army during the war, and later got a job as a driver with the Port Authority. Her mother never went to school, and even after twenty years in Abidjan speaks only the language of their village. Fortunately there are half a dozen families of the same tribe on the estate, forming a community within the community. Bernadette, the third child, grew up largely in this circle, with frequent visits to relatives in the village which is not too far distant.
>
> She must have been seven or eight before she started school. School is free, but uniforms and books cost money, and when a father has a large family to feed, he doesn't think about schooling until he must, or until perhaps a pay rise decides him. Seven is the average age of first year primary pupils. So Bernadette had a few years of formal education. But during this time the population of Abidjan was growing at a phenomenal rate – 200,000 inhabitants in 1960, and 350,000 in 1966. Although the Education Service was opening new schools fast, there was always a shortage of places. Bernadette was not the brightest of pupils (though let it be said that, unlike her mother *and most of us,* she can communicate in two different languages); she did not get to the top class of primary school.
>
> She was now, at thirteen or so, fitted for what? Village society would see her as a prospective wife and mother, and be satisfied with the prospect. Village society would also

provide plenty to keep her occupied for a few years, first helping her father at work in the coffee and cocoa plantations. The city held no alternative prospect, and no alternative occupation for the intervening years. There are many unemployed men; there are certainly no jobs for untrained girls. Bernadette could not share in her father's work as a driver. She stayed at home, to help her mother about the house and with her six younger brothers and sisters.

For her mother, this was of course a great help. But Bernadette had time on her hands and eyes in her head. In the village you don't see smart jewellery and attractive handbags. There are no cinemas or dance-halls just round the corner. In the city, the mere proximity of these things constitutes temptation. Young people, without work and without cash, turn, the boys to theft and the girls to the streets. It would not have been surprising had Bernadette gone the same way. That she did not can justifiably be attributed to the fact that she has Christian parents who care about her. Her most regular and most enjoyable occupation was singing in the church choir.

Then the almost inevitable happened. With nothing to do one evening, Bernadette and the boy next door (just left secondary school and going into the army) amused themselves together, and she had a baby. As is not uncommon, she became a mother before she became a wife. The boy next door has disappeared from the scene.

The church Women's Training Centre and typing school, designed to help girls with a limited education to improve on it, require a better standard than Bernadette's. The church primary schools, which form a valued part of the education service, are still a drop in the bucket. The church's answer to the needs of Bernadette and many like her lies, at the moment, in the local congregations, called to be communities in which young and old alike can find friendship and recreation, communities offering help to the tempted and pardon to the sinner.

Bernadette and her mother, who has just had another baby too, bring the children up together. The babies were baptized together. Before long, no doubt, Bernadette will be married, unless it happens again.'

In November 1972 we sent a circular letter with our Christmas cards. Here are parts of it:

'The 'development' of the Ivory Coast goes on apace. A big new hydroelectric dam has just been commissioned; the new port of San Pedro in the West is to be officially inaugurated next month; another fully-equipped 'tourist' village on an idyllic palm-fronded beach between the ocean and the lagoon is open this season; the other day several miles of dual carriage-way and spaghetti-type junctions were brought into operation in Abidjan.

The city's claim to be the wealthiest in West Africa is borne out by the need for such a road complex. We can testify to the increase in traffic. At one spot in town where until September you could drive straight through hindered only by the traffic-lights, there is now a jam at any time of day. Whereas we used to see traces of road accidents, or police measuring up, only two or three times a week, we now see at least a couple a day. There are many more televisions around too. When we came here in 1968 there was not one set on the whole housing estate. Now there are a good dozen houses where each evening you can see a crowd of children thronging round the door and windows trying to get a glimpse of some pretty rubbishy programmes.

But wealth is very unevenly distributed, and the principle that the man who has not will forfeit even what he has seems to work out quite well. One large shanty-town has been completely razed and new housing has been put up in its place. 'Of course,' went an official statement, 'most of those who lived here before do not earn enough to be considered for a tenancy.' So the inhabitants loaded their chattels onto carts, on their backs and on their heads and found a new site for a new squatter settlement. This is further from the sea and much less sandy, so water does not drain well and disease breeds fast. Now this area and several others are being cleared of all unauthorized building in their turn, since the government has decided Abidjan must be smartened up before Independence Day next August. The newspaper proudly prints photos of women weeping as the bulldozers move in, and points out that 'since the bulldozers were hired by the hour, no time could be lost letting people rescue their last belongings.' One article ended, with no trace of irony, 'In the end everyone benefits, except of course the people directly affected.' Meanwhile one newly-completed estate of good-class housing where 15,000 people have just moved in has no school, no clinic, no post office, an infrequent bus service – and the nearest shops are over a mile away.

Another aspect of the situation is that almost all of the people of the shanty-towns are foreigners. Ivorians always get priority both in housing and at the labour exchange, which means that many of the Malians and Voltaics who find jobs are exploited, unregistered and underpaid. The official attitude to foreigners is well illustrated by what happened when the nightwatchman at a factory was murdered two years ago and the safe robbed. The police arrested two Dahomeian employees at the factory, although the boss himself (a Frenchman) was convinced of their innocence. They still bear the marks of the brutal treatment they received, but after seventeen months they were released without trial and, as they were first-class workers, the boss took them on again. The Ivorians went on strike, refusing to work with 'murderers'. The Voltaics, realizing where their interests lay, joined in the strike. The boss was advised by the authorities not to re-employ the two, despite their innocence, in view of the 'psychological climate'…

The other day a member of our church here at the Port died. She had been ill for a year, and after an initial visit to the Methodist Hospital in Dabou, her family had insisted that she be treated with traditional medicine. Her husband, a clerk at the Port Authority offices, had no say in the matter; he finally persuaded them to let her return to the hospital when it was too late, and – as happens all too often – she died there.

When the news came, the church members piled into a lorry borrowed from the Port Authority and set off for her village, eight miles of muddy track beyond Dabou. It was a Sunday and John was taking a Harvest Festival in a fishing village. After the morning service, the whole congregation trooped across to the beach for a special prayer on the sea-shore – always an experience.

John then set out for the funeral, fixed for 4 pm, and reached the village just after the lorry, which had spent most of the day in a ditch five miles away!

It turned out that the customary meeting of the village elders to choose which cloths (the costly traditional dress) should be put in the coffin was only just beginning. Every man in the village had the right to speak and it went on a long time because the woman's paternal family and her maternal family (again, the husband was not included) were arguing about who had 'killed' her and they had to be reconciled … So by the time the brief church service was over and we had proceeded on foot, with chanting, to the village cemetery, it was pitch black.

In the night, the grave was found to be too small and had to be widened to take the coffin; the burial took place; we returned to Abidjan.'

CHAPTER 7

The All Africa Conference of Churches
(and associated memories)

The AACC was founded in 1963, when its constitution was adopted at an Assembly in Kampala, attended by delegates of over a hundred churches from forty African countries. A 1958 conference in Ibadan had set the ball rolling, but Kampala was the first official Assembly and the second was held in Abidjan in 1969. A team of 22 translators and interpreters was recruited to service the Assembly; ten were flown in from Europe, seven from elsewhere in Africa, and five of us were based in Côte d'Ivoire. There was no African in the team, which oddly did not strike us as remarkable at the time.

We worked in English and French. No-one came from Angola or Mozambique, still under Portuguese rule, or from Equatorial Guinea, recently independent from Spain. The Christian presence there – and in some of the Francophone countries – was largely, though not wholly, Roman Catholic and the Catholic churches were not members of the AACC. There was only a couple of RC observers, but Archbishop Amissah of Ghana gave a striking speech in which he suggested that Africa might give the lead in 'intercommunion'. He talked of 'a widening of the concept of apostolic succession on the part of some of us to embrace forms other than the imposition of hands by validly consecrated bishops'. It was acclaimed as an historic address, though it has sunk in the quicksands of time. I remember it well because I put it into French when the text arrived; I marvelled at the skill of the duo who had interpreted it, sight unseen, as it was delivered. Simultaneous translation was not really my forte.

I remember the Assembly too, because just at that time Pat went down with hepatitis. She was confined to bed, I was fully occupied, and Claire, then aged twenty months, went off to Agboville to stay with Judith Chapman and her two boys – Philip was interpreting in Abidjan with me. Judith took them to the market, hands held in line astern, and tiny Claire at the rear came home with a pocketful of fruit slipped to her by pitying stall-holders. After the Assembly I drove out to collect her and a stone shattered the windscreen, fortunately a rare occurrence even on the laterite roads. I had to push all the glass out, cover my nose and mouth against the swirling clouds of dusty particles thrown up by every passing vehicle, and arrived cloaked in red dust. Pat recovered in time to take our scheduled return flight home for an action-packed furlough, which included meeting two new in-laws – both my brothers had married that year in our absence – and adopting Paul.

Five years later the next AACC Assembly was held in Zambia. I was again an interpreter. I flew from Abidjan to Lusaka, via Lagos and Nairobi. I had a window seat as the overnight flight climbed out of Lagos and could see an array of red flares as we passed over the Niger delta. Natural gas, that could have been harnessed to fuel Nigeria's power stations, was going to waste. The oil companies had no incentive to make that investment and saved money by setting it on fire. I had seen it from close up when the Urban-Industrial Committee met in Port Harcourt. For fifty years pillars of fire have shot skywards, polluting the air with carbon dioxide.

Gas flaring in Nigeria.

The flight landed at Entebbe around 2 am. I roused myself and decided to get some fresh air, so I got off and walked with the handful of disembarking passengers across the tarmac. I headed into the transit area, bare and deserted. I had missed the announcement that transit passengers were to remain on board. After a few minutes I was challenged, and quickly confined to the stark departure lounge until it was time to board.

It was my first time in East Africa and my only experience of the tyrant Idi Amin's Uganda.

Among the issues to the fore at the Assembly was the conflict in Sudan. The AACC, especially its General Secretary the Liberian Canon Burgess Carr, had spent years building up trust with the government in Khartoum and the rebels in the south, and in 1972 brokered the Addis Ababa agreement which ended seventeen years of war. But already the mediators could see it was in danger of breaking down. In fact hostilities soon resumed and continued until South Sudan became independent in 2011.

Philip Potter preaching in Lusaka stadium.

Another item was the hotly debated proposal for a moratorium on missionaries, intended to allow African churches to find their own way independent of foreign missionary societies. Burgess Carr spoke vociferously and, some would say, intemperately, in support. Philip Potter, the MMS Secretary who had appointed us to Côte d'Ivoire, was by now the General Secretary of the World Council of Churches; he preached in the football stadium. He had taken note of the new clamour for inclusive language and his text never supposed that the term 'man' included women. Some of the French speakers, untroubled by the inclusivity of *l'homme*, found it tedious to translate.

The staff team was given a special perk. Half of us one day, the other half on another, flew down to Livingstone to see Mosi-oa-Tunya, the Victoria Falls. It was unforgettable. It was also, in those days, the furthest south you could go in Africa without compromising with apartheid. We took a river trip up the Zambezi past conventions of hippopotami, then turned downriver to view from afar the cloud of spray rising three times the height of the falls, the 'smoke that thunders'.

The Victoria Falls from the left (Zambian) bank of the Zambesi.

Another treat was in store after the Assembly. I had arranged to stay in Nairobi with Richard and Janet Collins. They met in Côte d'Ivoire, and got on well when they were with us one Christmas at the *Fraternité du Port*. Richard, I recall, arranged a party game and when it was my turn to imitate a creature of the wild I could not understand why no-one could identify the mosquito I was portraying until I was blue in the face with buzzing. It took me five minutes to realise that I was the butt of the whole game. Once married, Richard's accountancy took them to Cotonou, Nairobi, and for a spell to Amin's Kampala.

They had a long wait for my arrival in Nairobi. Tanzanian President Nyerere had been in Lusaka and was returning to

Dar-es-Salaam. To his credit he did not squander Tanzania's wealth on a private jet; on the other hand, he got the direct flight to Nairobi to make an unscheduled detour via Dar.

Richard and Janet gave me a wonderful weekend, typically doing with their visitor the things you never get round to on your own. We 'did' the Nairobi Game Park.

I wrote home:

'For the first hour we saw nothing more than the odd group of giraffe, ostrich and antelopes of various species. But then we came on large numbers of zebra, ostrich and wildebeest, and while we were parked just off the track observing them the nearest suddenly scattered and I spotted a hyena padding swiftly through the grass. We drove on through hordes of animals coming down to the water as it started to get dark and then, less than a mile from the gate, found a lioness on the road with a cub a few feet away in the undergrowth. It is amazing that there should be all that wildlife barely 20 minutes' drive from Nairobi, with planes passing low overhead all the time. The next day we drove through the Great Rift Valley to Lake Nakuru where three million flamingos mingled with storks, cormorants, pelicans and waterbuck. Can you imagine the perpetual noise? There was also a group of monkeys who played all over the car while we picnicked inside.'

Television wildlife programmes were not yet being made in those days, and in any case we had no television in Abidjan (the schedules did not warrant it!). So the real time experience was all the more special and memorable. Forty years ago, the plight of endangered species was not yet the hot topic it became. There were game reserves in East Africa, but elsewhere in the region predators and prey roamed freely, fed and bred undisturbed either by poachers or by cattle farmers with herds to protect. From Kenya I returned to the Ivory Coast: where, despite the country's name, the only sign of elephant I ever saw outside the Abidjan zoo was one steaming pile of dung, proof that a few still survived.

CHAPTER 8

A Journey to the Sahel

In 1972 I was awarded a small bursary from a now extinct fund to travel to Upper Volta – nowadays Burkina Faso – and Mali to visit some of the areas from which villagers had migrated to Abidjan in search of work, in order to appreciate better the tremendous adjustments they had to make on arrival in the city to the pace of urban life. I went with my colleague Samuel Traoré and with Philip Chapman, who had now moved to the new port of San Pedro. We went in the San Pedro Mission's Landrover. I was familiar with village life in the tropical rain-forest which formed the hinterland of Abidjan; this journey took us into the savannah.

We were immediately struck by how wooded the savannah was in this part of West Africa. We had expected grass-lands with occasional clumps of trees but found extensive stretches of woodland. The trees were not so tall, dense or of such girth as in the forest, but a lot of felling and uprooting was still necessary when ground was prepared for agriculture.

Cattle grazing in the Sahel.

Most of the migrant workers from this region spoke either Bambara or Mossi, but for many that was a second language.

There were, as in Côte d'Ivoire, numerous ethnic groups. We stayed in a Red-Bobo village, because it was Samuel Traoré's home, and a village of the Dogon tribe, a people reputed to be particularly resistant to the missionary religions, both Islam and Christianity. Both Bobo and Dogon migrants to Abidjan used Bambara as their vehicular language. Apart from Samuel's home we stayed with other missionaries. The protestant mission at work in both Bobo and Dogon areas was the Christian and Missionary Alliance (CMA). It was a bonus to learn something of their life and work. Both their theology and their missionary policy differed considerably from the Methodist line.

As the period of 'missionary power' came to an end, the CMA, in common with many missions of an essentially congregationalist ecclesiology, opted for a policy of 'separate identity' rather than for the integration of church and mission. An autonomous church was created; the missionaries, at least theoretically, had no say in the life of the church, and the church certainly had no control over the missionaries. Unlike Methodist areas, where even before the church became fully self-governing, whenever missionaries went on leave they could only return for another spell if they were officially invited by the local leadership. So while CMA missionaries could translate and publish the Bible, run bookshops and dispensaries and even Bible Schools, they could not preach or teach in the local churches without an invitation.

Another consequence was the complete financial independence of the African church. Methodists did not correlate self-government with self-support, and annual grants from Britain persisted after autonomy, although decisions about how to spend them were taken henceforth by the indigenous church. The CMA churches, on the other hand, had to finance themselves. Church workers, including ordained pastors, exercised a 'tent-making' ministry, which meant the church could give more attention to evangelism and less to money-raising for ministers' stipends. Yet separate identity also meant that in some places the African pastor lived in miserable accommodation right next door to the missionary's comfortable home.

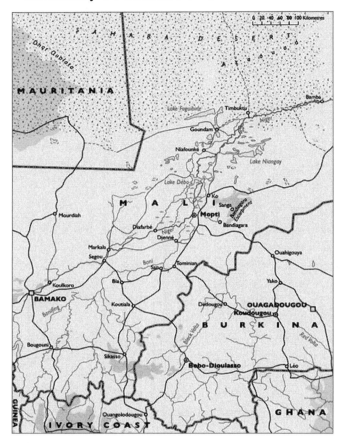

After three days on the road to Côte d'Ivoire's northern frontier, we reached Bobo-Doulasso, a name familiar as a station on the one railway out of Abidjan. The second city of Upper Volta/ Burkina, its name translates as 'the town of the Bobos and the Dioulas'. In comparison with Abidjan, it was scarcely a city. The bulk of the houses, even in the centre, were of the traditional flat-roofed mud type; there were few vehicles on the roads; and the quality of the merchandise on sale in the central market was poor – vast quantities of scrap iron, for example. The Bobo farmer made his own hoe, whereas his Ivoirian counterpart would buy a manufactured one.

From Bobo-Dioulasso we drove to Samuel's home, Dokuy, a village of two to three hundred inhabitants. All the houses were made of mud, whereas in a comparable Ivoirian village one would have expected to see several built of brick. But cement cost practically double the Abidjan price in Dokuy. Roofs were of mud rather than thatch. Doors had a wooden frame with a corrugated iron panel, since wood was in short supply. The overall aspect was squat and angular. There were villages with round huts in the area but they belonged to migrant Peulh and Mossi people.

When we arrived Philip and I were shown to a house where we would sleep – of course we had our Allisons camp beds with us. Our hosts noticed that daylight shone through several gaps in the ceiling – and it was possible there could be rain. They were

Roof repairs in Dokuy

quickly up the outside stairway onto the flat roof mixing mud and filling in the holes. It struck me how easy it must have been, in Capernaum in Jesus's day, to do the opposite and let a paralysed man on a stretcher down!

The Dokuy area was still relatively thinly populated. Everyone had fields within three kilometres of the village, where they grew millet, sorghum, corn, groundnuts, rice, fonio and chick-peas; they practised crop rotation with a fallow year. In contrast to Ivoirian custom, only men worked in the fields. At seed-time when we were there, they were leaving the village between 6 and 7 am and returning between 6 and 7 pm. But the women were not idle, hewing wood, drawing water, preparing meals and the lengthy processes of brewing beer and making karate oil. It was essentially a subsistence economy, but the quality of life compared favourably with many an Ivoirian village where coffee and cocoa could be grown for hard cash.

At the time, we learned, about two dozen people from the village had gone south, attracted by the reputed wealth of Côte d'Ivoire; it was unlikely that any would find themselves more comfortable than at home. Dokuy was six kilometres from the nearest primary school and rudimentary dispensary and thirty-two kilometres from the town of Nouna, where there was a well-equipped but poorly-staffed hospital, a post office and the administrative offices. There was no proper road across the savannah, but the tracks of the occasional lorry and the frequent donkey-carts were clear enough. The donkey-carts were a sign of real progress in the area. Prior to the 1960s, goods were carried on the donkey's back. Bicycles also became popular at about the same time, and most of the men now rode out to their fields by bike.

Philip and Samuel with the village chief.

We spent a day in Nouna, most of it with Mr Tyler, the American CMA missionary who had been there for over twenty years. His wife was away and he was ready to talk to us for hours. The best man at his wedding, he told us, was one Billy Graham – "Have you heard of him?" he asked.

We crossed into Mali, first visiting Djenné and its great mosque, on a platform some $75m^2$ raised three metres above the market place to prevent damage when the Bani River floods. There has been a mosque on the site since the thirteenth century, but the present structure dates from 1906. The walls were made of sun-baked earth bricks and coated with a plaster which gives the building its smooth, sculpted look. The walls of the building are decorated with bundles of rodier palm sticks that project about two feet from the surface. These are not only decorative but serve as readymade scaffolding for repairs to the erosion caused by the rains, which are effected by the whole community in the context of an annual festival. Djenné had not yet been declared a UNESCO World Heritage site. We were able to walk around freely; non-Muslims have only been banned since 1996, when the magazine *Vogue* held a fashion shoot in the interior courtyard and its pictures of scantily clad women outraged local opinion.

The great mosque, Djenné.

We continued to Mopti, a bustling river-port on the Niger. Picturesque in a rather ugly way, it is surrounded by water when the river reaches its height in the last quarter of the year and by mud-flats at other times. The guest room we stayed in had bats in the rafters. Our water filter appeared to have broken, until we realised that the water was so filthy that the ultra-slow trickle meant it was doing its job efficiently.

We had time to make a detour and look at the fabulous city of Timbuktu; we consulted a Catholic priest who described the route - we'd soon be off the beaten track and should follow the tyre-marks in the sand, at all costs avoiding the thorn bushes because their spines would wriggle into the inner tube ...

We spent a thirsty day in the desert, choosing at random

which tracks to follow when they diverged, and inevitably picking up a puncture. The sight of two dead camels did not encourage us to carry on. The Timbuktu visit was abandoned. We turned round. The spare developed a slow puncture. Stopping intermittently to pump it up, we limped back into Mopti.

The Dogon live on a rocky plateau east of Mopti. Refreshed and with new tyres, we drove to Sangha, at the top of the Bandiagara escarpment, taking two hours to cover the jolting last thirty miles. Here we saw what 'scratching a living from the soil' really means. There was rock everywhere and the smallest patch of earth in its crevices had to be cultivated. A variety of crops could be grown, as the protestant mission's garden demonstrated, but the dearth of soil meant the Dogon concentrated on millet, their staple diet. Those who lived at the foot of the escarpment, where houses clung to the cliff, were better off, with land on the plain for grazing and planting. No land was spared for burials; the dead were buried in caves in the cliffs, which could only be reached by means of ropes. The rope was made locally from the bark of the baobab tree, which thrives on having its bark stripped regularly. Caves were also used as granaries.

The cliffs of Bandiagara.

Bandiagara gets a lot of tourism. Sangha even boasted a motel of sorts, advertised in Paris travel agencies. That and walking tours of the area brought an income to the government and to the handful of people tourism employed, but no other benefits accrued to the place. It had simply introduced a materialistic morality and theft, we gathered, had become a serious problem.

At night we watched a colourful entertainment put on for the benefit of tourists – about half-a-dozen of us. In the morning we walked the steep path down the cliff. Our youthful guide pointed out some small and particularly inaccessible caves which he said were the dwellings of the Tellem people who had lived there from the tenth century until the invading Dogon drove them out. He described them as pygmies, but bones found there by anthropologists have all been of normal size. Those caves were probably never more than granaries and burial chambers.

On the second day we were there, the church was holding a day of prayer for rain, at the request of a group of non-Christian women. The early rains had failed again. Later that year the news became full of a 'seven year drought in the Sahel'; we were there in calamitous times, but had assumed it was their normal way of life.

It was time to return home, but we chose another route. We stopped briefly in the Burkina capital, Ouagadougou, then headed south into Ghana and found our way to Wa where we were welcomed by John and Jill Stedman at the headquarters of the Northern Ghana Methodist Mission. John showed us around the impressive School for the Blind. Most of its eighty-five pupils had gone blind from measles (there was a Roman Catholic School for the Deaf, again measles-related, in Wa too). I took away a letter dictated by a blind teacher and faultlessly typed by a blind typist. We noticed that another student, typing away, was producing nothing because the ribbon was not properly fixed; the teacher came and expertly replaced it in a flash. Thumbing through the School visitors' book, I noticed the signature of Tom Beetham, formerly the Missionary Society's Africa Secretary; when some years later, as Africa Secretary myself, I was again in Wa and visited the large new purpose-built School, I found that he had again preceded me!

We crossed back into Côte d'Ivoire – all our border crossings were uncomplicated – and drove through the Comoé National Park onto the road back to Abidjan. It was chastening to find the house had been burgled in my absence, but that only happened once.

CHAPTER 9

Three Weeks in Central Africa

The AACC asked me to lead a seminar on Urban Ministry in Lubumbashi in February 1975. Lubumbashi, the second city of Zaire (as the Democratic Republic of Congo was then known) was the centre of a rich mining area – cobalt, copper, tin, radium, uranium, diamonds. In the colonial era it was Elizabethville. At the time, my brother Bob and his family were living in northern Zambia, and on the map Nchelenge didn't look too far from Lubumbashi; it would be good to pay them a quick visit when the seminar was over. I duly applied for a visa for Zaire (I wouldn't need one for Zambia).

The embassy in Abidjan told me they had new instructions that all applications had to be processed in Kinshasa. "How long will that take?" "We don't know; since we started referring applications to Kinshasa we've not yet had a reply." I took heart from the fact that there were several diplomats applying at the same time, but when I returned a little while later I found that diplomatic passports had all been stamped, but mine was still waiting for authorisation. Furthermore, the airline had still not got my ticket, which the AACC was buying in Nairobi. I forget how many times I went to the embassy, but it all came together on the Friday before I was due to fly on Tuesday. I stopped at the post office to collect my mail from the box and there was a message from the airline to say they had the ticket, and I went on to the embassy where they handed me my passport with the visa.

Snag. I had asked for a transit visa – twelve days en route to Zambia, when I would do the work, and two days on the way back, simply to get back to Kinshasa and catch my flight home. But no: I'd been given one week in each direction. Could they change that please? No: I'd have to go to the Bureau des Affaires Etrangères when I got to Kinshasa. Another snag. All foreigners had to prove they'd spent $40 a day while in Zaire (which I'd have more than done had I bought the plane tickets between Kinshasa and Lubumbashi myself, but they'd been bought by the AACC). As a 'guest of the church' I could get a certificate of exemption signed by an authorized church leader. The snags were only just beginning.

I had written to a Swiss contact, Olivier Dubuis of the Evangelical Theological School in Kinshasa, asking him to meet me on arrival and arrange somewhere to stay until I flew down to Lubumbashi after a couple of days. No reply had come and I boarded the plane that Tuesday with some trepidation. I was delighted when Fritz Fontus joined the flight at Libreville. Fritz was a Haitian friend; he had been the Bible Society representative in Abidjan. He would have not have abandoned me friendless at the airport, but happily my letter had not gone astray. I was met and hosted by the Dubuis. The certificate of exemption proved easy. The United Methodist bishop, who lived 1000 km away, chanced to be in the capital. We had a useful conversation and he gave me a certificate. I realised there was no way I could get my visa changed. I phoned Pastor Nshid, the seminar organiser in Lubumbashi, and they decided to bring the date forward.

The distance from Kinshasa to Lumumbashi is not quite 1,000 miles, roughly equivalent to a London-Lisbon flight. When I arrived I was told that the participants would be coming in the next day. The United Methodist Church in Shaba province (which these days has reverted to its former name, Katanga) made radio contact with all its superintendents at noon each day; no other form of communication was reliable. They'd all been alerted to the change of timetable. I would not have the time I'd expected to look around, interview people and generally get the measure of the urban context in which they were ministering. I was, yet again, in at the deep end. A dozen participants turned up, some ministers and some lay, from the mining towns of Lubumbashi, Likasi and Kipushi.

I needed to be gone on Tuesday. Zaire under Mobute Sese Seko was not a place to outstay your visa. There was a minibus service to Chililabombwe in Zambia at 9 am. I left the seminar with a last exercise to tackle and made it to the bus station in time, then sat until 11 am before the driver decided to set off. He then drove to a bakery to collect lots of bread with which he would bribe his way past the numerous military road blocks. We reached the frontier at 1.30 pm.

At the frontier they wanted my certificate of exemption. I pointed out that I'd need it when I left from Kinshasa, but I had to hand it over. "Collect it when you return," someone said. I was more than doubtful, but the bus was ready to leave so I'd have to cross that bridge later. In Chililabombwe I looked for a bus to Nchelenge. I'd catch one from Mufulira, I was told, so I took a bus there to find I'd been wrongly informed. The thing to do was to go to Kitwe and catch the bus next morning. I did: found a hotel, got an early call, was at the bus station, as advised, at 4.30 am, and eventually left at 6.30 am. In those days the route north took us across the pedicle, the south-eastern strip of Zaire that pokes into Zambia, so there were more frontier controls as well as a ferry across the Luapula river, and a couple of police 'everybody out' checks. We arrived in Mansa at 2 pm and were told the bus would depart at 5 pm. When we got on the road again, the reason for the long halt became evident. The bus had been given a complete service, and it needed it before venturing onto the bone-shaking road. There were fewer passengers now, and we all sat in the front seats as the red dust swirled to the rear. A notice prohibiting bus drivers from consuming alcohol was cheerfully ignored by the two drivers, swigging beer. We drove on through the dark, and I was set down at the gates of Nchelenge Secondary School at 10 pm.

'Dr Pritchard, I presume' was the obvious greeting when I finally located the correct staff house. I was a week earlier than expected. Bob and Liz never received the letter I wrote telling of the change of date, nor did I get the one he had sent saying he would meet me at the frontier, but to get home he would have to leave at 1 pm. The bonus for him was that he only had to make the journey once, when driving me back to the frontier, and for me the bonus was not only that I met my niece Jo for the first time but that I was there in time for her second birthday. She and her big sister Becky looked after me when Bob and Liz were teaching.

The return journey began well. At Zambian road blocks Bob cheerily introduced me as 'my father's first-born' and we were waved through. I said goodbye and walked back into Zaire.

As I thought, my exemption certificate had disappeared into an untraceable bureaucratic drawer. I caught the bus back to Lubumbashi. I gathered that the bishop was now home in Kanenge, midway between Lubumbashi and Kinshasa, quite inaccessible. Pastor Nshid, the Lubumbashi Methodist minister and convener of the South Zaire Urban Ministry Committee, who had chaired the workshop, had no certificates to sign. And when I tried to reconfirm my ticket to Abidjan that flight number didn't exist. Throughout the trip I was spending half my time on organising my next moves. However, I was able to discuss the conclusions and recommendations of the seminar in depth with Pastor Nshid, and I had a very good day at the Methodist University at Mulungwishi, some hundred miles away, the oldest private higher education institution in the province, where my lectures to theological students had been deferred from the previous week.

Back in Kinshasa, I lectured at the Theological School, where ministers of ten protestant churches were being trained. Crucially I managed to reconfirm my flight; the number on my ticket was the one to which it changed when it got to Libreville. And mercifully Olivier Dubuis had a spare exemption certificate signed by the bishop. He'd signed two for a recent visiting couple, but as a couple they'd only needed one!

All the snags were overcome. I'd done all I went to do and Pat met me in Abidjan at precisely the time I was expected. She never got any of the postcards I sent her; but towards the end of March I got a letter posted on 26 January containing the famous $40 exemption certificate …

CHAPTER 10

Family Fragments

Claire and Paul were able to start school at the age of four, unlike their playmates in the Cité du Port who would not enrol until they were six or so. The Ecole des Petits was a private kindergarten and primary school, a short drive from home. The children's 'bush' French improved rapidly and they were happy there. We took the decision to return to Britain not because of the language, but because the French educational system differed markedly from the English. We were aware that to switch a few years later could be a real setback.

Claire, John and Paul in the garden.

Whenever we came back to England on leave, people would say, "You live in Africa – you're not very brown," to which the reply was "We're not so foolish as to go out in the blazing sun – we stick to the shade."

Nevertheless Claire and Paul got plenty of fresh air. When they were out in the compound, neighbourhood youngsters would drift in to join them. Often enough small toys, particularly cars, would depart when they did. Such items were not a priority for most family budgets. Yet the local children displayed considerable ingenuity in making their own playthings. In many parts of Africa I have seen little cars or bicycles, made from twisted lengths of wire, being steered around village streets or yards. At the Cité du Port, it was more than likely that the wire had been snipped from our perimeter fence!

Dressing up for the school gala.

Missionary families were blessed by Madame Kozah, a Lebanese member of the congregation on the Plateau. She bought and wrapped Christmas presents for every child. Unwrapping them was a great treat. But in their earliest years Claire and Paul were just as happy with simple things. My brother Colin once sent a set of empty yoghurt pots and a couple of table-tennis balls. Coupled with a basin of water, these kept them amused for hours.

The port was being developed rapidly when we moved to Abidjan. The container revolution was just beginning. Dredgers worked night and day, and a mile of quay – eight or ten extra berths – emerged from the lagoon. Alongside the docks, a new road ran south towards the coast. This made it quick for us to drive down to the sea, near the mouth of the Vridi canal, which we used to do most weeks at the end of an afternoon. I would often go wearing no more than swimming trunks and a pair of sandals, but incongruously carrying a briefcase. Its contents included the identity cards and driving licences that had to be with us at all times, in case we came across a police check.

The new quay.

These documents were invaluable. More than once, when stopped for speeding (only slightly above the limit, of course), the officer would check my ID and say, 'Ah! Vous êtes missionnaire. Allez doucement.' (Go carefully). No bribe forthcoming from that driver, he well knew. But on the one occasion my parents came to visit us, returning late from a dinner date, we were stopped at a flying checkpoint on the new road. I had our documents but I had forgotten to remind my father to take his passport. After a lot of discussion, and still no bribe offered, Pat was allowed to drive home and get it, leaving the rest of us at the roadside. On her return, it appeared that the passport had not been stamped with the date of arrival in the territory. If that were so, it was clearly the fault of airport security, not my father's. The patrol was determined to extract something from us. But they failed. They finally let us proceed around 1 am.

From the beach we gazed south. Beyond the horizon, the equator was 400 miles away. The nearest land, 1,500 miles off, was St Helena, where Napoleon ended his days. The view of the waves surging in cannot have changed for many millennia. It could be rough, but it was usually safe to swim. However one day I emerged and discovered that my wedding ring had come adrift. I often wonder whether it was ever washed up and now adorns some other finger, or whether it is still tossing around in the ocean.

Atlantic breakers.

On another occasion when I must have gone in shorts the house key slipped from my pocket into the sand. This I discovered when we got home. Breaking into my own house proved quite difficult. I didn't have a saw handy to saw through one of the wooden slatted windows. Eventually, after several attempts, I managed to batter my way through the toughened glass window of the downstairs toilet. At that point our nightwatchman arrived. "What are you doing?" he asked. "What you are employed to stop anyone doing," was the answer I bit back. We always entertained a suspicion, maybe unjustly, that nightwatchmen paid a bribe to the local burglars and then slept the night away.

For a while we kept guinea-pigs, enclosed by wire netting in the back garden. Several times their young disappeared overnight. Jean, the groundsman, said they'd been taken by a snake. We suspected they'd been poached for food. This time the suspicion was unfounded, for one morning Jean called us to see the snake he'd just killed. The corpse had two small guinea-pig shaped bumps.

We had a papaya (paw-paw) tree just outside the back door. It grew from seed at an astonishing rate. After no more than six months it was as high as the bathroom windows upstairs and was soon bearing fruit. Vegetation in the tropical rain belt sprouts even more  quickly than the weeds in our Sussex garden. Luigi, an Italian friend, was a wood buyer. One day he took a party deep into the rainforest to see a tree felled. It was a Sunday and I couldn't go, but Pat took the children. When they got there, the woodcutters had already erected scaffolding around the enormous roots.

Standing on it they had been attacking the trunk with axes since daybreak. The shudder and noise when it fell was alarming. That day the family left early and got back very late. I was getting worried. It was what Pat felt times without number when I returned late from some venture.

Denis and Léa were two young friends. I met Denis when I was leading Bible Studies at a Technical Institute. They were both charming and asked me to marry them. Pat picked up a second-hand wedding dress for Léa when on leave. Church weddings were unusual and I was concerned because, although Léa had a child, the couple had not yet begun a family. In fact they never did; a rare example in that culture of an infertile marriage enduring. They were devoted to each other. At one stage Denis had a breakdown and was sectioned in the psychiatric hospital in Bingerville. I remember taking Léa out to visit him when his disturbance was at its worst. It was heart-breaking to see him in that state and in those surroundings. But Léa was strong. Denis recovered and later became an accountant in the church headquarters, while Léa became a national Women's Work leader.

Friends both African and European: we were sorry to bid them farewell. I had the good fortune to return to Abidjan as the Missionary Society's Africa Secretary over a decade later and caught up with some of them, including Denis and Léa. Others, long since dispersed or deceased, remain lodged in our memories.

CHAPTER 11

Harris Creed

We returned to England in 1975. I wrote this piece for the Overseas Division's *NOW* magazine the following year. It appeared in May 1977. I no longer remember if the punning title was my own or the editor's!

'When the Liberian evangelist William Harris was expelled from the Ivory Coast early in 1915, bringing to a close his remarkable missionary crusade, he left behind hundreds of village congregations dispersed throughout the southern part of the country. Some of these groups soon became part of the Roman Catholic Church; most rejected the overtures of the priests and suffered ruthless persecution from the French colonial administrators.

It was almost ten years before Methodist workers began to follow up Harris's mission, making contact with these scattered communities and organizing them into a church. It is not surprising that many of them were by that time unwilling to accept white oversight and leadership. Only after a French missionary had sought out Harris in Liberia, and returned with a message from the old man and a precious photograph of them shaking hands, were they persuaded – and even then not all of them.

Pierre Bénoît greets Harris, 1926.

In 1929 Harris was visited by another delegation from the Ivory Coast, including a certain John Ahui from a small village near Abidjan. It appears that they received a blessing from the dying preacher, who was happy for them to carry on his work independently of the Methodists. John Ahui became, and remains, the head of the Eglise Harriste, the Harrist Church. Most of the congregations which rejected the Methodist take-over are loosely connected with this church, though some reject Ahui's leadership.

Features common to all Harrist groups are the distinctive white clothes worn by men and women alike for attending services, the use of large numbers of candles in church (even where electricity is available), the architectural style of the brick-built churches with their twin towers, and the use of traditional indigenous music – airs, rhythms and instruments. It is the height of discourtesy to cross your legs during a Harrist service, and there is a special church steward to keep an eye open for offenders (and not averse to prodding the uninitiated visitor!).

The relationship between the Harrist and Methodist Churches has always been cool. During the pre-independence period it was complicated by political factors, and the Harrist Church, proud of its freedom from all European influence, gained in strength. Since independence, however, the situation has begun to change, and while there are still virtually no official contacts between the two churches, there are increasing links at the local level. In some places the two congregations (or even three, with the Catholics) will worship together at certain festivals; during a campaign in the new town of San Pedro I was privileged to preach at a Harrist service. More significant is the way in which Harrist and Methodist preachers occasionally share together in sermon preparation classes, and one or two Harrist preachers have attended ten day local preachers' conferences. This is not always welcomed by the Harrist hierarchy and they have sometimes risked expulsion. But there is a new literate generation growing up in the Harrist Church and as the Bible is read more widely, rather than kept unopened as a fetish on the altar, it is sure that there will be more and more points of contact with other Bible-based, though leg-crossing, churches!'

The last paragraph was probably more optimistic than the situation warranted. My colleague Emmanuel Yando had contacts with Ahui and the Harris Christians, but I think they came to nothing. When the Ivory Coast District became a fully-fledged self-governing Church in 1984, he became the first President. I suspect that his preoccupations thereafter left him no time to build on those earlier relationships.

CHAPTER 12

Return to Ghana

In 1975 we left Africa and for the next ten years had no occasion to return. I worked first in Sheffield and then in Portchester, at the head of Portsmouth harbour, where Methodists and Anglicans worked well together. One of our shared projects, spearheaded by a former British ambassador to Sudan, supported Voluntary Service Overseas, who asked us to sponsor a VSO nurse in Ghana. I became a member of the Methodist Africa Advisory Group and in 1985 was asked to join a small team representing the British Methodist Church in a consultation with the Methodist Church Ghana. It seemed a good idea to tag on a visit to Hannah and the Ghanaians were happy to arrange this.

Most of the British team had African experience, but some of us had forgotten just how hot and humid it would be. I remember how at the first opportunity after landing in Accra we were vying with each other to stand in front of an air-conditioner! The consultation held its first session in Accra before we moved to a conference centre in Nsawam. Several Ghanaians referred in their opening and welcoming addresses to 'the mother church' in Britain. This was too deferential; we saw the consultation as between equal partners, each with our own strengths and weaknesses. Albert Mosley, the General Secretary of the Overseas Division (as the Missionary Society had become) was quick to respond, 'Sometimes we think we are the grandmother church, and grandmother has lost her teeth'. The point was taken, and set the tone for a constructive meeting. It was facilitated (like a similar consultation held in Sierra Leone the year before, and a third due to be held in Nigeria in 1986) by a trio of skilled enablers, George Lovell, Leslie Griffiths and the Jamaican, Ivy McGhie.

The primary objectives of these consultations were to learn, together and from each other, how to be most helpful to each other in our respective contexts and how our work might be enriched in partnership and fellowship through exploring common problems, concerns and resources. We attempted to establish guidelines for determining priorities for mission and for the use of resources. The Catholic Conference Centre in Nsawam was a good place to meet – had we remained in Accra some of the Ghanaians would inevitably have been distracted by 'pressing' calls and absented themselves. But in days long before the advent of mobile phones they were incommunicado! The living accommodation was sparsely furnished: no sheets on the bed, we simply lay on the mattress, which was OK in that climate. Only when we were leaving did those of us sleeping on the top floor discover that the rest had proper bedding and that our floor had simply been forgotten.

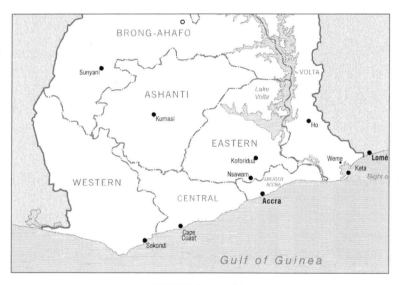

GHANA (south).

Back in Accra for the weekend, I excused myself from the programme arranged for the others in order to go to Wemé, near the Togo border, where Hannah and two Canadian volunteers ran a clinic. The church generously offered me a car and a driver. The driver kept me waiting patiently – no, impatiently, I imagine – and it was late on Saturday afternoon when we set out. I forget how far we had gone when we had our first puncture. It took a while to change the wheel, and at the next town it took a good hour for the tyre to be repaired. Not much further, and a second puncture. Eventually, a third. We stopped, just short of a village. Clearly the driver would have to stay overnight with the car, or it would be vandalised. What was I to do? We ascertained that there was one car in the village, but its driver had had an injection and wasn't fit to drive – at least, that's what we were told. Nothing for it but to return to the roadside and try to thumb a lift. Vehicles passed occasionally. It was a long wait before one stopped.

There were two occupants. The driver in a smart suit and bow tie, his companion in a T-shirt. They knew where the clinic was and were happy to take me. In fact they were more than happy, they were exceedingly merry. They were returning from a wedding in Accra and were much the worse for drink. As we careered along the coast road, they burst into song: *Will your anchor hold in the storms of life ... we have an anchor that keeps the soul.* Lines not at all in keeping with their state, and the tune not exactly on key. But by God's grace we arrived safely at the clinic. Around midnight, we roused the nurses who had long since given up on me. Around 2 or 3 am, they were roused again by the sound of me vomiting violently in the guest room ...

With Hannah at Wemé clinic.

On Sunday I was shown around and we went to the beach. Way back I had stayed in the government rest house in nearby Keta, when en route to a meeting in Lomé. Now the place was unrecognisable. With much of the town it had been swept into the sea. But there was a nice beach at Denu with warm sea-breezes.

On Monday the driver arrived with the car. He'd spent Sunday taking a bus back to Accra, where he kept a brand new spare tyre under his bed! He must have given some youngsters money to keep an eye on the car until he got back. He didn't ask me to reimburse him. We returned to Accra, and to England, without further incident.

A couple of months later I was interviewed for the post of Africa Secretary. At lunch before the interview the chairman of the panel said, "Do you remember when you brought Desmond Tutu to see me?" Indeed I did.

Bill Knowles had spent a year in Abidjan before going on to teach at the Seminary in Porto Novo. Tutu, not yet so well known as he became, was working for the Theological Education Fund. I had been asked to escort him on his visit to Côte d'Ivoire. This sort of thing happened because I lived not too far from the airport, and spoke English.

Thirteen years later, Bill was chairing the Appointments Committee. I do not suggest for a minute that our previous acquaintance got me the job.

My adventures in Africa were only just beginning.

CHAPTER 13

Nyaminyami

The book of Revelation begins with 'letters to the seven churches'. The Africa Secretary's work consisted of correspondence with the seventeen churches!

At that time three of them, in Benin, Togo and The Gambia, were still administered by the British Methodist Conference. Seven were autonomous Methodist Churches that had grown from work begun by British missionaries: Sierra Leone, Côte d'Ivoire, Ghana and Nigeria on the west coast, Kenya (with outposts in Tanzania and Uganda) in the east, Southern Africa (with work in six countries) and Zimbabwe in the south. In Zambia the Methodists had helped to form the United Church and in Equatorial Guinea there was a loose federation with the Reformed Church. Much more recently, relations with the Presbyterian Church in West Cameroun had been established, and there was a tenuous link with the Kimbanguist Church in Zaire. Each of these had their own concerns to share; in many the Overseas Division was supporting British workers and a few had sent ministers to serve in Britain under a partnership arrangement; all were in receipt of funding, in the shape of annual contributions to their general budget or occasional grants for specific purposes; they had the opportunity to nominate students for bursaries in Britain that had to be vetted. There was much to learn and more than enough to keep me fully occupied in London, but in my second month I was dispatched on a visit to Zimbabwe.

In 1985 the Division had addressed a letter to partner Churches around the world, enquiring whether they were planning any evangelistic initiatives among peoples untouched by the Christian gospel, and asking whether the co-operation of MCOD would be helpful. Almost at once a reply came from Zimbabwe. The arrival of the letter coincided with a recommendation from Morris Maswanise, a Zimbabwean minister, to develop work among Tonga people living on an arid plateau south of Lake Kariba.

The then President of the Church, Caspen Makuzwa, visited the area in May 1986 and it was agreed to explore the possibility of a joint venture. Recognising the immense practical human needs as well as the almost total absence of organized Christian activity, it was thought that a team ministry with evangelistic and humanitarian dimensions would be called for. Two of us were sent to investigate further. I was very glad that on my first official visit I had the company of my colleague, David Cruise.

We arrived on the same overnight flight as Robert Mugabe, returning from the UN General Assembly. We could not disembark until after the Welcome Back ceremony but that went fast. He shook hands with the entire diplomatic corps in under two minutes. The jacarandas were in full purple bloom in Harare, and the roads were carpeted with fallen blossom. A few hours later there was a light shower, the first rain for several months. We were told this was a good omen: 'When the chief comes, he brings the rain' according to local folklore.

Many conversations with various people about issues of church (and state) occupied the rest of the day, and whenever occasion arose in the days to come. On my first visit south of the Zambezi I had many questions to ask, and people had plenty of questions, requests and stories for the new Africa Secretary. But we were there primarily to take stock of Nyaminyami, and next morning four of us set out on the long drive north; Caspen Makuzwa and his successor Farai Chirisa, David and I. A good tarred road brought us to Karoi in time for lunch where John Millns, a septuagenarian bachelor, veteran of 12 years in Madras and 15 in Rhodesia, was expecting us. He gave us a slap-up meal of roast beef and Yorkshire pudding, apple pie, strawberries and ice cream, and coffee grown in his beautiful manse garden. Another four hours rattling on dirt roads brought us to Siakobvu, the Nyaminyami District Centre. There was no habitation at this spot, until a police post was established in the 1970s. A clinic and a store followed, and the small administrative complex was very recent. The 'multi-purpose training centre' where we stayed – dormitories, kitchen and classroom, no electricity – had been completed only four months previously.

Nyaminyami the river spirit.

For the Tonga people, living on the banks of the Zambezi, Nyaminyami was the name of a river spirit, with a snake's body and the head of a fish, residing in the Kariba gorge. When the Kariba dam was built in the late 1950s the Tonga reluctantly allowed themselves to be resettled away from the rising lake waters. They believed that the building of the dam deeply offended Nyaminyami and attributed the regular flooding and many deaths during its construction to Nyaminyami's wrath. The Tonga on the southern, Zimbabwe, side honoured their new home with the spirit's name.

We stayed in Nyaminyami from Thursday evening until Monday, touring the area and having discussions with District officials. Morris Maswanise and his wife had come from their home, fifty miles away, to ensure we were comfortable and fed (we'd brought provisions with us from Harare). Morris was held in high esteem by all we met, and thanks to his spadework the four local chiefs were united in inviting the Methodist Church to extend its work in their area. In Siakobvu itself there was no school, but I visited the library, built with Canadian funds. Most of its shelves were empty, but it held twenty copies of Wuthering Heights! On our drives around the area we called at several primary schools, all technically day schools but with mud-built 'boarding houses' erected by children who lived too far away to go home each night. They cooked for themselves after school and went home every week or two for more food. In one school the head boy was the chief's son, a Christian aged about 18, who said he hoped to become a minister; during term-time he stayed in a boarding house while his wife and two children lived with her family – marrying so young was quite normal.

In another school we were entertained by a 'marimba consort' – the instruments were crammed into the head's small office, the only lockable building in the village. In another I saw an English exercise on the board: 'Yesterday was Sunday and we go/went/ going to church ... The Bible readings were writing/wrote/written by Matthew and Luke.' The nearest church of any kind was at least seven miles away. Long journeys on rough roads were normal. Women were walking twelve miles each way to get their corn ground at the grinding mill and had to do it every three days. Shortly before we arrived two people had died at the roadside trying to get to the Siakobvu clinic; the bus from Harare came through only three times a week and wouldn't carry seriously ill passengers, and there was no ambulance in the District.

On Saturday we drove north to the lake. A mile after passing through the Tsetse Control post, where the pick-up was liberally sprayed, the cab was invaded by tsetse flies.

Although we wound the windows up fast, I got several irritating bites. The irritation wore off quickly, but I made a note to myself that if early in January I were to struggle to get up in the mornings it would no doubt be sleeping sickness (thirty years on I don't have that excuse!). Flies were the least interesting wildlife we saw that day. From Bumi Hills (a plush hotel with its own airstrip, where we indulged in iced drinks) we observed a large herd of buffalo on the sandy lake shore, several elephant out on an island, some waterbuck and a Bateleur eagle hovering overhead. From the nearby fuel depot (our reason for this detour) we saw hippo bathing and a fish-eagle sat motionless on a tree-top, its eerie cry echoing across the water now and again. On the way back to Siakobvu, several bushbuck close to the road, then a small herd of elephant that we stopped to observe through the undergrowth.

Between us we led Sunday worship at three places, small congregations gathered, one in a rudimentary shelter with a single plank slightly raised on stones to sit on, another in a school classroom. Here I preached and Morris interpreted in Chitonga. At the time I could probably have reckoned up into how many different languages my sermons have been translated over the years; to my regret I have long since lost count.

Later in the day we sat down to discuss our findings and draw up some proposals for developing work in Nyaminyami. Back in Harare, at a meeting of the President's Council, Farai asked me without notice to report on our visit. Fortunately I had been drafting a report for MCOD earlier in the day so my mind was clear. The Council was happy with the proposed package. It recommended that a Zimbabwean minister be stationed at Siakobvu; that MCOD provide the funds to build a manse with a solar lighting module, a four-wheel drive vehicle and if necessary a grant for the minister's children's school fees, such as was made to missionaries based in places where no suitable education was available locally. We would also fund the provision of a mobile clinic, seek to recruit a qualified nurse-midwife and provide her housing; the Provincial Health administration would fund a Zimbabwean counterpart and a driver. The President's Council was of course a Methodist body, but the President of the

Republic was keen to hear what we were proposing when we visited him at State House. In those early years of Zimbabwe's independence, Mugabe was Prime Minister and the President was Canaan Banana, himself a Methodist minister. He offered us a cup of tea and a scotch pancake and gave us his position on ridding South Africa of the apartheid régime: 'Comprehensive mandatory sanctions are needed'.

David Cruise and I now went our separate ways. After a few more days acquainting myself with Zimbabwe, meeting more of the church leaders and some of the British and Irish mission partners, Farai and Gladys Chirisa took me to the airport. The flight was delayed because of fog at Gatwick – no point in leaving Harare on time and then circling for hours over southern England waiting for the fog to lift. We eventually boarded long after midnight and a few minutes later heard the rumpus of a motorcade. Robert Mugabe was flying with me again.

A postscript: a few weeks later an experienced nurse-midwife, Deina Smith, made an offer of overseas service and was promptly assigned to Nyaminyami. When she first arrived her house was not yet completed and she shared not only a home but a bed with her Zimbabwean colleague for some weeks. Morris Maswanise himself volunteered to pioneer the ministerial appointment. Some time later we arranged for him to spend a few weeks in Britain, to tell of his experiences. He made a powerful impression, not only by what he had to say, but because throughout his stay he steadfastly refused to drink more than six glassfuls or mugfuls of liquid a day. If he got used to more he would suffer when he returned to Nyaminyami where water was carefully rationed.

CHAPTER 14

Nigeria

There were no mobile phones, text messages or emails in the 1980s. Nor could you compile a blog when you were travelling abroad. I kept a journal and compiled a report later. I reckoned that for every week away, it took a week's hard graft to catch up on the backlog of work awaiting me in the office on Marylebone Road. Getting back from Zimbabwe I knuckled down to it and then, a month later, Nigeria beckoned. I had been there once before, to a meeting of the West Africa Urban-Industrial Committee in Port Harcourt in 1974. I'd even been in police custody there, after taking a photo of an anti-aircraft gun. Fortunately both I and the camera were released unharmed. This time it was to attend the third in the series of consultations with West African Churches, to be held in Ibadan; I had been part of the British team in Ghana a year before and now I was there ex officio.

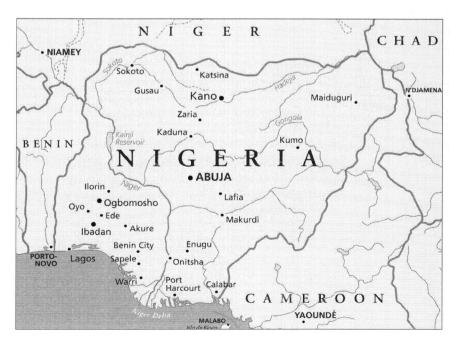

Albert Mosley, the General Secretary of MCOD, should have led the team as he had at the previous consultations, but he could not get a Nigerian visa because his passport had a South African stamp in it. Nigeria was not doing business with people who had business with the apartheid regime. Although Albert explained that he had been to South Africa in solidarity with black enfranchisement and not in cahoots with the oppressors, his application was flatly refused. Even though, he argued, the imprisoned Nelson Mandela was a Methodist. I realised this would be a problem for me and so I applied for a second passport, which I obtained without difficulty. I could now visit either country as long as I remembered which passport to present. And it fell to me to lead the delegation to Nigeria in Albert's stead.

The Nigerian team was led by Bishop Rogers Uwadi, whom I had already got to know. Almost my first task when I started work at the Mission House was to meet him at Heathrow one Saturday morning. I drove him to his hotel, just round the corner from Marylebone Road, where we were told that his room would not be ready until the afternoon. So I drove him out to our home in Croxley Green, where we were still settling in. Pat was ironing curtains when we surprised her. Rogers was easy to entertain. He kicked off his shoes and curled up on the sofa with his Walkman, still in his full Episcopal regalia.

Clerical dress had taken a striking new form with the indigenisation package introduced into Nigerian Methodism in 1976. Its architect was Bolaji Idowu, who had torpedoed the Nigerian Church Union process in 1965 and then split the Methodists when he pushed through a new church order, headed by a patriarch – the office to which he was himself inducted in a nine-hour ceremony where he was presented with golden keys, the symbol of his authority. A sizeable minority, mainly in the East, objected and seceded.

British and Irish Methodism were left in an uncomfortable position. Most Methodists looked askance at the elaborate hierarchy, the hotch-potch of titles – the Patriarch was to be addressed as 'Your Pre-eminence' – and the lavish outlay on vestments. The Overseas Division was continually lobbied, particularly by former missionaries in the East, to side with the minority faction which had retained the old constitution. The Division declined to take sides. The dispute had to be settled by Nigerians. But for a decade relationships were cool, communications infrequent.

Things began to change when Sunday Mbang succeeded Idowu in 1985. Mbang was bent on resolving the conflict, and already peace meetings were being held in the dioceses. He did not take part in the Ibadan consultation, any more than did the President of the British Conference, but he came up from Lagos to share in the opening and closing sessions.

It was an opportune time for the consultation, even though the mains water was off at the Pastoral Institute in Ibadan; each morning we all trekked down to the water tank in the yard to fill our buckets, then back upstairs for a cold shower. In our discussions we were able to remove misunderstandings and misgivings on both sides. The unhappy history of strain between the two churches was acknowledged. It was a step on the path to the reconciliation of the two factions which was eventually achieved in 1990. Most of the titles and regalia were maintained, but Patriarch became Prelate, 'Your Pre-eminence' became 'Your Eminence'. Sunday Mbang was a skilled and tireless operator.

Returning from Ibadan to Lagos, the British team were invited to lunch with the Mbangs. I had more business to do. MCOD had recently launched a new scheme. From its inception the Missionary Society had determined that all fund-raising should be for its general fund, which would be allocated by its committees who were best placed to decide priorities. There would be no special pleading, no special collections for special interests. Of course this principle had not always been respected, but of late there had been a clamour for identifiable targets to focus on. 'Second Mile Projects' were invented.

The first mile was still to ensure enough income to meet all the Division's budgeted commitments; the second mile, for congregations who chose to take it on, would be for a project submitted by a partner Church. As well as raising money, there would be literature helping people to understand and empathise with the situation. At this juncture MCOD had suggested that it would attempt to raise £75,000 for a project or projects in Nigeria. After lunch Sunday Mbang took me aside to think about the right cause to support.

There were many possibilities. At the consultation I had for the first time met Ros Colwill, the enterprising Welfare Officer at the Uzuakoli Leprosy Centre, still being re-established after five battles had been fought across the compound during the civil war. There was an ill-equipped Motherless Babies' Home on the adjoining compound. There was the hospital at Ituk Mbang, where my cousins the Cundalls had spent their childhood, which had – not for the last time – been taken over by government, run into the ground and handed back to the Church. The needs of these humanitarian ventures were clamant and I had no doubt that £75,000 could be raised for any of them. But Sunday had already made his mind up and was not to be deterred. He wanted the whole amount to go to building a church in the new town of Abuja, destined to replace Lagos as Nigeria's capital in 1991.

I subsequently visited Abuja a couple of times. In 1988, when the place consisted of miles of broad highways, but little in the way of buildings apart from the gleaming new mosque, the Second Mile Project had been successful and the construction of the church and manse was under way. I shared in a confirmation service. There was a congregation of a few score and a small Boys' Brigade company. By 2008 that first little building was now part of the Methodist primary school and at the top of the compound, built entirely with Nigerian contributions, stood a great 'Cathedral of Unity' with a great congregation. Sunday's instincts had been right.

METHODIST CHURCH NIGERIA
ARCHDIOCESE OF ABUJA
THIS CATHEDRAL WAS DEDICATED
TO THE GLORY OF GOD
BY
HIS EMINENCE SUNDAY MBANG (CON)
PRELATE METHODIST CHURCH NIGERIA
ON SATURDAY 3RD MAY 2003
MOST REV. S. OLA. MAKINDE
ARCHBISHOP OF ABUJA

On my visit in 1988 I spent two weeks seeing Methodist work up and down the country. As usual my itinerary was arranged by my hosts and I was left in no doubt that my concerns about the Church's medical work were amply justified. I was taken to visit Uzuakoli, Ituk Mbang and Ama-Achara hospital in the East, and the former 'Wesley Guild' hospital at Ilesa in the West.

In Britain I was an ex officio member of the national Wesley Guild executive. The Guild, with numerous branches in churches nationwide, had sponsored the hospital in Ilesa from the outset in 1913. But the Wesley Guild Hospital had been taken over by the government in 1975, and from 1987 it was part of the Obafemi Awolowo University Teaching Hospital Complex. The Guild in Britain sent books for the Library of the Nursing School on the occasion of the hospital's 75th anniversary, but links had become tenuous. In the executive we discussed a new initiative, which eventually matured as the Nigeria Health Care Programme. I am fond of saying that I was in at the conception, but not at the birth, of NHCP, for by the time it was launched I had left the Africa desk. But not before I had toured Nigeria again.

In the course of my visit in 1991, I was taken to see two maternity hospitals, at Ikole and Omuo, both back under church management after ten years of neglect under state control. At Ikole on a Saturday morning there was no outpatient clinic and the sole task of the day was to discharge the only inpatient and her new-born baby. My escort, Bishop Ayo Ladigbolu, told the parents to name him John in my honour! At Omuo – where the Methodist church had a congregation of 2,000 – the hospital had only two deliveries in a month. One of the two original buildings had burned down while in government hands and was left in ruins. Many years later in Croydon I saw a presentation about the Nigeria Health Care Programme and suddenly recognised that the first of two 'before and after' pictures of Omuo was one I had taken. Over twenty years the NHCP raised a million pounds and assisted thirteen hospitals, clinics and health centres, three centres for mentally ill homeless people, the leprosy centre and motherless babies' home, an eye clinic and an orphanage.

I saw some of these when I travelled with a NHCP delegation

in 2008. I particularly wanted to see a venture that had been planned on my watch two decades earlier. Amaudo was a home for destitute homeless people with mental illness. It was the brain child of Ros Colwill.

I spent a couple of days with her in Uzuakoli in 1988 and marvelled at all the activities she oversaw, not a few of which she had instigated. There were three 'Grainger villages' (named after their original British sponsor, Lila Grainger) where leprosy sufferers lived, a variety of rehab workshops, the elementary school, farm, a printing press, a 2.5 hectare rubber plantation being tapped daily, and an oil-mill processing home-grown oil palm. Most of the workshops had a supervisor and a varying number of trainees who lived in the rehab village and received a very small training allowance. After two years they were given a little equipment to go home and set up business. They were producing comfortable artificial limbs; sandals – mostly sold at a subsidised price to residents for whom proper footwear is so important; bricks, for the settlement's own rebuilding programme; roof-tiles, simple to make and to lay, attractive in appearance and cool; cabinet-making; weaving cloths and presbyters' stoles; and, for those too ill or deformed ever to return home, a sheltered workshop doing cane crafts such as wickerwork chairs and trays. Some of the residents had formed their own co-operative which was running a little store on the spot and a small soap-making operation.

The following year Ros came home on leave and sat in my office excitedly sharing her vision of a centre for people with severe mental disorders. The leprosy victims with whom she was working were outcasts. Here were more outcasts, so deranged that their families could no longer care for them, unable even to say where their home once was. They were to be seen begging on the streets of every town. Some of them were chained, abused, forced to beg by cruel gang masters. Ros's ambition was to provide a home for them, where they could receive care and treatment and be helped to recover at least some degree of mental health. She received the blessing and backing of my colleagues and committees and so 'Amaudo' – meaning Village of Peace – was born. Only those who had lost all contact with their families were admitted.

Ros Nkechi Colwill.

In London I saw the plans of the complex: accommodation for fifty or sixty residents, workshops, dining room, common room, offices, built in a circle around the chapel which was the focus of the community. But I had never seen it personally. Since then Ros had been seriously ill following an infection which left her with a hemiplegia and near blindness. I visited her in Oxford when she was in intensive rehab.

Eventually, against the odds, her faith, her resilience, her spiritual resources got her back to Nigeria where she became a spiritual director and established a Retreat Centre on the Uzuakoli campus.

Uzuakoli in 2008 was very different from the hive of activity on which I reported twenty years earlier. Apart from caring for a few very frail old people, the leprosy work was done: a success story. The others had all gone back into village communities, no longer shunned. Amaudo looked just as I had envisaged it from the initial drawings, though a bit run down after nearly twenty years. Ros, though still dependent on two carers, was known and respected throughout the region; despite pain and impairment, she remained a delight and an inspiration.

CHAPTER 15

Southern Africa's Six Nations

January 1987 was cold. Particularly cold in Uppsala, where I attended a meeting of the European Liaison Group of the Programme for Christian-Muslim Relations in Africa – the name was almost as long as our agenda. The giant thermometer in the middle of Uppsala read minus 21° at 1 pm! I called on Professor Bengt Sundkler, a well-known scholar of African church history and author of *Bantu Prophets in South Africa.* He put to me a thesis which I have often quoted: *The first missionary was never first*, wherever a foreign missionary arrived some other believer(s) had invariably paved the way.

A few days later I set off for South Africa myself, and to a very different climate, especially when I got to the sweltering humidity of Durban where the Chairmen of all the Methodist Districts were meeting (they were not yet styled Bishops, and they were all men).

I first landed in Johannesburg and packed an astonishing amount into the next two days. One of the first people I met was Peter Storey, Chairman of the District, who had prepared his opening greeting knowing full well it would be repeated in my reports: *Welcome to fairyland!*

South Africa, governed by the small minority who were of European stock, was under a State of Emergency. I heard dozens of stories, many tragic, some absurd, about the injustices and cruel treatment suffered by the black majority and I met a lot of people whose names were well-known in the anti-apartheid movement of that time. I had been part of the movement in Britain ever since the Sharpeville massacre of 1960 had prompted the campaign to boycott South African produce (one of the ironies of this visit was to enjoy the fruits that at home I had avoided for years).

I was on the executive of Christian Concern for Southern Africa. I was well briefed. But now I was able to meet people on the front line of the struggle. A morning at the offices of the South African Council of Churches with Beyers Naudé and his colleagues, and a visit to the Methodist Community Centre in the vast black suburb of 'Soweto' (an abbreviation of South West Township), filled out the picture for me.

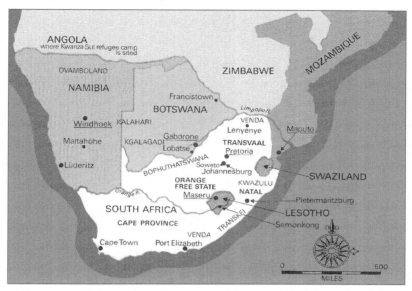

Southern Africa – showing some of the so-called 'homelands' of apartheid South Africa.

Wherever I went, politics inevitably dominated my conversations; it impregnated every area of life. But there were diversions. When I got to Cape Town, as well as seeing some of the squalid townships and catching up briefly with Desmond Tutu, I took the cable-car to the top of Table Mountain with its splendid views and admired the botanical specimens on the slopes.

Cape Town and Table Mountain.

When I returned to Jo'burg at the end of a whistle-stop tour, a visit to a goldmine had been arranged at my request and I was taken down Cooke no 2 shaft in Randfontein, all the way to the bottom at 1,300 metres below ground. At 970 metres we took a train for about a mile and then started mountaineering. Mr Duplessis, the supervisor who was my escort, had 560 black miners and drivers in his section; they produced 35,000 tons of ore a month yielding 4.5

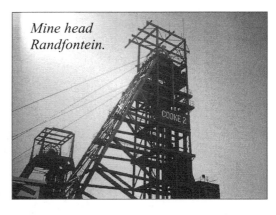

Mine head Randfontein.

grams of gold per ton – though he pointed out one seam which had yielded 20 grams. The miners, at the end of each cramped and filthy shift, returned to the single-sex hostels in which they were corralled.

After my initial orientation period in Johannesburg, I went to Lesotho. Semonkong hospital, up in the highlands, was the only place in Southern Africa where MCOD had sent missionary personnel for many a long year. It was opened only four years earlier and had still not established itself – I was told that people would always prefer to go down to the lowlands for treatment, where they could shop and do other business at the same time, especially now that a decent new road had reduced the journey time from seven hours to two. It was a magnificent drive: many people on horseback, heavily-laden donkeys, flocks of sheep and smaller numbers of cattle, the occasional bus, people wearing blankets and hats reminiscent of Andean scenes, a cool wind blowing when we reached our destination at 7,300 feet. Dan Senkhane, the superintendent of the Lesotho mission with whom I was staying, delivered a replacement water pump which was soon working to everyone's delight. I was sorry not to spend more time in Lesotho – I have never been back – but after two nights it was time to move on. Others were waiting for me.

Next stop, back in the Orange Free State, was Thaba N'chu. It was only years later that I came to realise how large it loomed in Methodist history; James Archbell was a pioneer missionary among a branch of the Tswana people who, back in the 1830s, were constantly on the move, harassed by Ndebele and Zulu warriors, far from the present Botswana. He obtained from the Sotho king, Moshoeshoe (pronounced Mosheshwe), land at Thaba N'chu where he and they settled. The manse was a historic monument; the first white child in the Free State was born there. In 1987 it was the plight of black children that pre-occupied me. Close by was the vast Botshabelo relocation area, where six or seven thousand people, expelled from their homelands under the Group Areas Act, had been dumped. The Act reserved the most fertile land and prosperous urban areas for whites. Deposited in Botshabelo, a dispossessed family found a tin toilet and a shabby tent, and was left to build their own shack. I was taken to visit an elderly woman who lived with three grandsons, significantly not at school, in a tiny shack with only a table and a broken park bench for furniture. And to a graveyard full of tiny graves.

It would take too many pages to relate all my encounters which came thick and fast. Many discussions centred on economic sanctions, boycotts and disinvestment. Some of those I met opposed them, but in the circles in which I moved, most, black and white alike, considered them the last chance of effecting change peacefully.

After a couple of nights in Bloemfontein, I flew down to Port Elizabeth and it dawned on me that wherever I went, apart from Lesotho, I was staying with white households. I asked if I could stay somewhere in New Brighton, the black township. I was told that given the racial tension it would be dangerous, not only for me but for my hosts, and had to accept the answer. Of course all my white hosts, in Grahamstown, East London, Cape Town, Durban and back in Johannesburg, were hospitable and informative, but I determined to meet a wider community next time.

Next time came later in the year. There was an important ceremony in Namibia to which I was invited. I flew into Jo'burg and was met by the Soweto minister, Sizwe Mbabane. Whereas on my first visit my itinerary had been wholly organized by the Church headquarters, this time I arranged it myself. As we drove into Soweto, Sizwe explained, "I have arranged for some community leaders to come round and meet you this evening." The first to arrive was Winnie Mandela. Her husband had by this time been transferred from Robben Island to Pollsmoor prison in Cape Town; she herself had been regularly detained by the South African government, subjected to house arrest, held in solitary confinement for a year, tortured, kept under surveillance and was still at the forefront of the struggle for inclusive democracy. The British Consul-General also came. The evening was all too short as I had to be up at 4 am to catch my Friday morning flight to Windhoek.

Demetris Palos, known to all as Jimmy, met me at the airport, 25 miles from Windhoek. Half-way back to town, he ran out of fuel. He flagged down the airport bus (driven by a Methodist) and told me where to find a phone booth at the bus terminal. I called his office and was soon taken to the manse, while his wife Daphne went off to rescue the stranded Jimmy. A lesson learned before we set off on two thousand miles of driving over the next five days!

After lunch we set out on the first 300 miles and were up at 5 next morning for a further 200 miles: our destination was a barren spot in the far south of the country where in 1825 three missionaries were murdered. The Africans, Jacob Links and Johannes Jager, and the Lancastrian, William Threlfall, were buried by local KhoiSan (bushmen) where they died, and their graves were rediscovered

Namibian martyrs' memorial.

in 1986. A monument was erected on the spot and I was asked to unveil the commemorative plaque. Several hundred people came – four busloads from Leliefontein in South Africa, the mission station from which the trio had set out. The ceremony began five hours late because the two buses from Windhoek, with choirs on board, had a succession of problems. Each of the graves was marked with a cross and in between stood a stone monument featuring a V for Vriede – the Afrikaans for Peace. My contribution was almost the only element in the ceremony which was not in Afrikaans.

The Windhoek party spent that night in a schoolroom at Warmbad, the nearest town, and after an early service with seven choirs we spent the rest of the day driving back. A short detour took us to Mukurob, or Finger Rock, a sandstone monolith balanced precariously on a conical shaped pile of rock debris formed by erosion. It had stood for millennia, but the next time I passed that way in 1989 it had collapsed.

Mukurob.

After a night in Windhoek, it was another long drive north to Rundu on the Kavango river which forms the border with Angola. Civil war and South African occupation made Angola a disaster area; there were some 50,000 displaced Angolans around Rundu and the majority of Methodists in the Kavango Mission came from the 'Portuguese' sector.

The South African Defence Force was stepping up its activity in Angola and one conscript recently killed at the front was a Methodist minister's son. Earlier in the year I had heard, from his parents, about another young white man who had made up his mind not to do military service. He therefore had to choose between a year in prison, six years of community service – still part of the apartheid system – or going into exile. Apartheid was nasty and vicious, never more so than in what proved to be its waning years.

I flew back to Jo'burg and on to Swaziland, where I spent a night before proceeding to Mozambique in an old Dakota with no hold and no luggage racks, all our baggage stowed at our feet. Mozambique, like Angola, had been in the grip of civil war ever since the Portuguese left and here too South Africa was backing and supplying the rebels. Of the eight ministers in the Mozambique District, one had lost his wife in a rebel attack, one had lost his leg and a third had lost his brother, captured in a raid three years before and not heard of since. Amid another packed programme what stands out is an afternoon at Nkasana, a ten-minute ferry-ride across the bay from the capital, Maputo.

It was somewhere near here that William Threlfall went down with malaria in 1823. In his delirium he wrote a note to the captain of a ship that had just sailed into the bay, 'Please come and bury me. I died at 2 o'clock this afternoon.' He recovered, only to be killed in Namibia two years later.

The church at Nkasana was the oldest Methodist building in the country, and looked it: a large, high, airy building, all the more airy because of the holes in the corrugated walls and roof, and between the floorboards which were raised a couple of feet from the ground. At a recent minister's welcome service a section of the floor collapsed beneath the weight of a packed congregation.

Although it was a Friday afternoon, over 300 people turned up, including a well-practised youth choir. I was presented with a wood carving and then it was the young people's turn. "We can't do much," said their spokesperson, "but we'd like you to have something so we've made a cake." Eating it later with Isaac Mahlalela, the District Chairman, and his family was a sacrament.

I still had another country to visit. In Botswana I stayed with Jennifer Potter, geography teacher at Gaberone Secondary School and also Vice-chair of the Botswana Christian Council.

The highlight here was to accompany Jennifer and the General Secretary of the Christian Council to Etsha in the northwest of the country. This was where some 4,000 Hambukushu refugees from the fighting in Angola had come to an area, recently cleared of tsetse fly, on the western side of the Okavango delta. The Christian Council had from the beginning been involved in their resettlement, supplying emergency food aid and later seeds and implements for self-supporting agriculture to begin.

An Anglican priest, Father Ronald Wynne, was concerned that only material aid was being given. He saw the need for a spiritual ministry to these people, largely illiterate and ignorant of Christianity, and in 1970 he was appointed by the BCC with an ecumenical mandate: to bring the Hambukushu to Christ without introducing denominationalism. He lived among them for seven years, learning their language and culture, producing a Thimbukushu dictionary and literacy primers, and telling them Old Testament stories which likened their experience in fleeing from Angola to the Exodus event.

After seven years he mentioned Jesus for the first time and a few months later 350 people were baptised by full immersion in the Okavango pools. With the birth of a church that had no denominational ties, there followed much heart-searching and intense debate in the Council (in which Roman Catholics were full members) about the celebration of the Eucharist, self-support and kindred matters. Father Wynne retired in 1981 and was succeeded by a team of two Methodist couples, one from New Zealand and one from the USA, and Catrien Meijers from Holland, the only member still there in 1987.

The Etsha Christians themselves agonized over their identity and in 1985 chose a name for themselves, 'The Liberation (Mashutwero) Church of Jesus Christ'. They were not accountable to the BCC, but its officers kept in regular touch, and it was a privilege to join them.

A two-and-a-half hour flight across the Kalahari desert in the Flying Mission's six-seater Cessna – one seat removed to make space for all our luggage and supplies – brought us to Maun, where we touched down and refuelled.

We flew low over the Okavango Delta, which gave us stunning views of buffalo and unidentifiable antelope, lots of herons and a crocodile. We buzzed Catrien's house, then surveyed the airstrip carefully before landing. Catrien and a group of Hambukushu were soon out to greet us.

There were thirteen villages in Etsha. Catrien lived in the largest, Etsha 6. The Mashutwero congregations all met for worship under trees; their only building was a new meeting house, called 'Keheyu' (meaning Everybody) which had just been completed in time for our coming. There were lots of meetings for Everybody that day!

Later Catrien took me for a drive; she seized the opportunity to talk with a sympathetic but independent outsider about some of the issues that taxed her. The church had selected its own leaders. The question was whether some should be ordained and if so by whom and by what rite.

One stumbling block was the Thimbukushu practice of plural marriage – Father Wynne admitted polygamists to baptism and communion while upholding the ideal of monogamy. Catrien said, "They know the difference between a good marriage and a bad one; that a good marriage means fidelity, caring and bringing up the children well; and (a telling point) that plenty of monogamous men sleep around." At Easter the leaders, though unordained, had celebrated the Eucharist themselves. Mr Mmono, the BCC General Secretary and a Roman Catholic, took the news calmly and commented – as one might when a girl got pregnant, said Jennifer – "Well, it's happened, hasn't it …"

We flew back to Gaberone next morning, in time for Jennifer's two lessons after break. Over lunch the BBC World Service broadcast the news of the great October 1987 hurricane that had struck the south of England. I scuttled round to a neighbour who had a phone and ascertained that our house – and greenhouse – were standing. Next day, back to South Africa for the start of the Methodist Conference in Benoni, with a powerful open-air service on Sunday morning and later an ordination service in the air-conditioned Civic Centre with a congregation of 2,200, at which I read a lesson.

I had been away for three weeks. It was time I headed home to clear up the debris from the storm.

CHAPTER 16

Sierra Leone

I went to Sierra Leone twice, in 1987 and 1990. This was before Foday Sankoh's Revolutionary United Front, backed by the brutal Liberian warlord, Charles Taylor, and financed by blood diamonds, sparked a ruinous eleven-year civil war, but the country was already in dire economic straits.

My first objective on any overseas visit was normally to acquire some local currency. In Sierra Leone, regulations required that foreigners exchange at least £60. I stuffed my holdall with packets of brand new notes, more than many a Sierra Leonean would earn in a year. The exchange rate was 80 leones to the pound. At independence in 1961 it was 2 leones, when I returned in 1990 it was 320 leones, in 2015 it is 6,700. In Freetown in 1987 those people with bank accounts were having difficulty getting hold of cash: the banks were short of notes, presumably because most of the money was at the airport! Making ends meet was, on that visit, the primary topic of conversation. Both the European mission partners and, to a desperate extent, the local church personnel, were struggling to cope with inflation. It was heart-breaking to visit two retired schoolteachers with nothing but their pension to live on, a pension whose purchasing-power had collapsed.

Prior to independence, Sierra Leone consisted of 'the colony', the small western area around Freetown, and 'the protectorate'. The population of the colony consisted chiefly of descendants of freed slaves, whose ancestors originated in many parts of west Africa. They speak Krio, derived from English but with influences from some African tongues and Caribbean idioms. The peoples of the interior have their own languages and customs, including the Mende, the largest group in the south-east of the territory. My time was divided between Freetown and the Mende area. That involved a lot of travelling, and fuel was in short supply.

The country's economic problems took off in 1973 when oil prices quadrupled, Sierra Leone being entirely dependent on fuel imports. When I arrived in 1990, an oil-tanker had just started discharging at the refinery, after spending ten days anchored in the bay under instructions not to come alongside until its oil had been paid for in hard currency. On Saturday night a long queue of vehicles had formed outside every filling-station in Freetown, hoping for fuel on Monday morning; in fact it was the following Saturday before the pumps opened, and the customers were rationed to two gallons each. Unsurprisingly some people had taken to stockpiling fuel. That was dangerous. I saw the ruins of a house that had recently burned down. The insurance, inadequate anyway because of inflation, was forfeit because the owner (an MP) was storing petrol there.

Sierra Leone produces no oil, but it is rich in minerals, especially diamonds. The thought of a quick fortune had lured great numbers of peasant farmers away from their lands to prospect in the area around the town of Koidu, which had mushroomed from a few huts to the third largest population centre in the country. Most of Sierra Leone is fertile and sunshine and rainfall are abundant, but so many cultivators had abandoned their plantations that agricultural production had plummeted. It should have been a net exporter of rice, but on my first drive into the interior I saw lorries not taking rice down to Freetown but rather bringing imported rice inland.

The church was running several agricultural projects, the largest at Tikonko with forty employees, including the staff of the workshops in Bo producing small handtools, beehives, bellows, and a cassava-grater that was unusable because it ran on diesel. There were some keen, enthusiastic staff members, but there was much to disappoint. The farm manager showed me thirteen rabbits – "We used to have two hundred until a tree fell on the hutch and they got away"; the well – "We had a pump, but it's not working, so we draw water by hand"; the fish farm, a small pond with no fish "because it dries up by the end of the dry season"; vegetable plots abandoned because of the constant depredations of village animals.

Other elements of the project were functioning, but the failures seemed to arouse no anger, no vision, ambition, imagination other than the temptation to pack up and go prospecting for diamonds.

Prospecting for diamonds.

It was the same when I visited the Bunumbu Press run by the United Christian Council, which had a long and productive history. I found it had been idle for two years. Of its three large type-setting machines, the linotype came second-hand and never worked, while another had been cannibalized to keep the third going, but that was useless without paper. There were stacks of pages of a Mende hymn-book in the binding room, waiting for other pages to be printed. The literacy manuals on the shelves, and the Mende translation of Rip Van Winkle (!), were covered in dust and I got the impression of a very low turnover.

Even at the hospital in Segbwema the operations on the day I arrived had been cancelled because all the surgery patients had infections. The laundrymen had been hauled over the coals. The theatre block was well equipped, but the autoclaves were broken; a solitary Tilley pressure burner was heating one, and that had already been repaired at least once.

On that first visit I was taken, over appalling roads, as far as the eastern frontier at Koindu bordering on both Liberia and Guinea. I met some extraordinary people working hard and well, whatever the odds. There was as much to impress me as to depress me.

When I got back to Freetown I went to the Christian Council offices one morning to share a multitude of conflicting experiences and check out my perceptions with some of the staff.

Then it was time for their weekly act of prayer. I was still brooding when we stood for a hymn.

We sang:

'Though vine nor fig-tree neither their wonted fruit should bear,
Though all the field should wither, nor flocks nor herds be there,
Yet, God the same abiding, his praise shall tune my voice,
For, while in him confiding, I cannot but rejoice.'

Resignation or resilience? I had seen both on my travels. And I remembered that my colleague David Cruise once told me that he had asked an old man in one of the villages above Freetown, "What's your favourite hymn?"

The answer:

'Why should I complain of want or distress,
Temptation or pain? He told me no less.
The heirs of salvation, I know from his word,
Through much tribulation must follow their Lord.'

Both those hymns date from the eighteenth century, when Freetown was still being settled and before Christian missionaries arrived in west Africa. They expressed the faith of the beleaguered Sierra Leoneans 200 years later in a way which the trite ditties of 'contemporary' worship songs cannot match. They knew much tribulation; and much worse was to follow. In the course of the 1990s, civil war displaced two million of the country's six million people, with some 490,000 fleeing to Liberia and Guinea, while the unspeakable atrocities committed by the insurgents have been well documented.

In 1987 HIV/AIDS had scarcely appeared on the scene, while Ebola, though first identified in 1976 when there were two small outbreaks in the Sudan and Zaire, was unknown through all the years I travelled in Africa. On the other hand, Lassa fever, which also had high mortality rates, was endemic in the region. Pioneering studies of Lassa fever had been done at the Nixon Methodist Hospital in Segbwema by Dr Isabel King and Dr Aniru Conteh, who at the time of my visits was the hospital superintendent – when civil war broke out, he and the Lassa Fever Unit relocated to Bo. But, for all their fearsome impact, Ebola and Lassa were never such major killers as malaria and tuberculosis.

I sat for an hour one evening on the veranda of a doctor's house in Segbwema, deep in conversation. The mosquitoes were biting furiously, in spite of the bug-repellent anklets I was wearing. At the end of our discussion I remarked, "The mosquitoes are out in force tonight." "Are they?" he replied, "I haven't noticed them."

Clearly the blood of a visitor was more attractive than the blood of a resident. But only the irritation troubled me. I was at no risk from malaria, since throughout our time in the Ivory Coast and on my subsequent journeys I always took a prophylactic and if, occasionally, I couldn't sleep under a net I kept a mosquito coil burning. Few Africans had such protection. The moves to make impregnated mosquito nets widely available are of more recent date.

There was an excellent TB service at Nixon. Patients were required to pay the charge for the twelve months' course of drugs up front, in order to avoid the common situation in government hospitals where treatment could be abruptly halted if a patient ran out of funds – which rendered the entire treatment ineffective. Even though in Segbwema they had paid in advance, some failed to complete the full course because of the high cost of travel from home to hospital. The charge was heavily subsidised by the hospital, and with TB on the increase that aggravated the sorry plight of the hospital's finances.

Nixon Hospital received a pathetically small government grant, and only a handful of staff were supported by MCOD. Drugs could only be had for hard currency and the exchange rate put them way beyond the means of most patients. Indeed, the registration fee was barely enough to pay for record cards, let alone a consultation. To raise fees enough to balance the books would make it a hospital for the élite or, more likely, reduce patient numbers to an unviable trickle and close it down altogether. Such were the dilemmas with which I was confronted at the Africa desk, and especially in Sierra Leone where infant mortality was one of the highest in the world and, by 1990, life expectancy had fallen to a mere 35 years.

'Be of good courage for man's disappointment is God's appointment.'

I concluded my report of the 1990 visit thus: 'I marvel at how life goes on, and good work is done, and people keep cheerful, and their faith burns bright. I cannot imagine what the future holds. There are no precedents for what happens to an economy when it reaches this state.'

CHAPTER 17

Equatorial Guinea

The island of Bioko, known throughout colonial times as Fernando Po, occupied more of my time as Africa Secretary than its size might have warranted. The Roman Catholic Church was the dominant Christian influence when it was a Spanish colony; Primitive Methodists arrived in 1870. At independence in 1968, the island was united with the mainland colony of Rio Muni to create Equatorial Guinea; the new country's capital was Malabo, formerly Santa Isabel, on the island. There were communities of Presbyterians and of the Worldwide Evangelisation Crusade (WEC) in Rio Muni; some of their members were now working in the capital and the Methodist plant in Malabo was shared with the separate Presbyterian congregation.

Macias Nguema, the first President of the Republic, democratically elected, proved a brutal dictator. He not only forcibly merged opposition parties with his own and made himself President for life of both nation and party, he forcibly merged the three Protestant churches into one: the Iglesia Reformada (IRGE). Until 1973 the Methodist Church was under the Nigerian Conference and the majority of Methodists were Nigerians, migrant workers on the cocoa plantations. Macias terminated their contracts and the Methodists who remained numbered little more than a hundred persons in three congregations.

Macias was overthrown by his nephew, tried and executed in 1979. The three Protestant communities re-asserted their autonomy and for years argued over property rights. I was summoned to a meeting in Geneva in 1987 and met Samuel Oké, the General Secretary of IRGE and acting minister of both the Malabo congregations, together with a few Europeans who were endeavouring to resolve the disputes and to assist the under-resourced churches. They spoke warmly of the Methodist leadership. I needed to see for myself.

It began inauspiciously. After a fortnight in Nigeria, I flew to Doula, where I was supposed to be in transit, but the Equatorial

Guinea football team had just been thrashed by Cameroun and they and their supporters, 34 of them, had commandeered the Malabo flight. A dozen regular passengers like myself were left stranded and angry.

Since it was only a thirty minute hop to Malabo I asked why the plane couldn't come back for us. Apparently there was no radar at Malabo airport and by this time darkness was falling. My suitcase, checked through to Malabo, had flown; the one saving grace was that they radioed through and when the plane returned the case eventually re-appeared.

I was given a 48-hour visa to stay in Cameroun – though the next scheduled flight was 60 hours away, which I was told wouldn't matter! The airline gave me 24 hours at the Falaise Hotel, which provided good meals and a swimming pool, and a voucher for a taxi to return to the airport next afternoon.

Next morning, Tuesday, I managed to call Samuel Oké from the Post Office and explain my predicament. I spent the afternoon at the airport trying to ensure a priority seat on the Thursday morning flight, but there were no guarantees. I had to do the same on Wednesday afternoon – we were only given a day at a time at the hotel and another taxi voucher. I spent my time reading, writing my Nigeria report and swimming. But on Thursday we flew, in a 17-seater Twin Otter that Equato-Guinea airline had acquired from Air Madagascar – the safety instructions were printed in Malagasy.

I was met by Samuel and the wondrously-named Juan Macfoy Barleycorn, scion of two of the first Methodist families. Since I was scheduled to leave on the weekly Iberia flight to Madrid on Saturday morning, I had to cram all I'd come to do into less than 48 hours and forgo a quick visit to Rio Muni.

I was taken to pay my respects to the Catholic Archbishop and to the Minister of Justice and Church Affairs. I inspected the Methodist compound, with a church and primary school. The attractive manse had been commandeered by Macias as a guest-house. After he was deposed, the church was given two flats over a disused shop as very inferior compensation. I went to Baloeri, a small village with a large, but never-full, church and some decrepit buildings which had been a school in the 1930s. Here I met old Mr Sipoto, whose son James was a minister in Nigeria; I had met him in Calabar and discussed his returning to Bioko. And I spent a long time discussing the needs, resources, budget and constitution of the Methodist Church. IRGE-fusion, as they called the shotgun amalgamation, had at last been formally dissolved. I'd be doing more work on this in the coming months. In fact with my input over the years to the statutes of Methodist Churches in Côte d'Ivoire, Bénin, Togo and Portugal, I've been a consultant on constitutions in French, Spanish and Portuguese – I can't hold a conversation in Spanish or Portugese, but I could work my way through legal documents!

The old and empty manse at Balekia.

I returned to Bioko twelve months later. I again stayed with Emilio, another of the Barleycorn clan. James Sipoto had come and I inducted him on Pentecost Sunday. We visited two more Methodist outposts, neither very far, but lengthy drives owing to the state of the roads. In Luba, the island's second town, Emilio pointed out the prison where he had been badly beaten and held for four days under the ousted President Macias, for protesting when his goats and pigs were seized. He was Secretary of the Chamber of Commerce at the time, but that did not spare him. There were more discussions about the constitution and, with the Presbyterians (who had shared fully in Sunday's worship), about ongoing property disputes. On my last evening there was a meeting with the 'Women's Auxiliary' who turned out in force – at least fifteen of them, though I couldn't count as we met by hurricane lamp and candle-light. Electricity was supplied in Malabo every alternate 24 hours and water came through the taps for an hour or so each morning.

After that Emilio took three of us for a drive which ended up at the Bakaya, a bar on a government campus. I wandered past a raucous group dining – by candlelight of course – on the patio, to have a look at the swimming pool, which turned out to be dry. One of the diners decided this was suspicious behaviour. He was the President's chef-de-cabinet, much the worse for drink, and had Emilio and me detained.

It later turned out that a Moroccan delegation had been staying in government guest-houses on the compound and the previous day important documents had been stolen from one of them. I think the chef-de-cabinet had been hauled over the coals and he was now demonstrating his assiduity. He made the Lebanese proprietor of the bar drive the two of us to the central police station, where we were left to kick our heels. Emilio was trembling; I'm sure he was reliving his experiences in Luba. A policeman from the Bakaya bar rang up to tell the duty officers the story, which made them laugh but brought us no relief. Our molester had gone off, probably intending to leave us stewing there until the morning. But the proprietor tracked down another Presidential aide who turned up well after midnight and ordered our release; we were marched out of the station at the double.

Meanwhile our two companions, who had avoided arrest, called Samuel Oké, and he in turn had contacted the President's chef-du-protocole, who was one of the Presbyterian elders. We had not long been back at Emilio's when the chef-du-protocole turned up with a personal apology from the President who had been personally informed of our plight.

After a very short night it was early to the airport. Our tormentor was there, but we avoided any confrontation. I flew back to Cameroun and on to Zaire, where more adventures awaited me.

CHAPTER 18

The Kimbanguists

The Church of Jesus Christ on Earth by the Prophet Simon Kimbangu was the largest of all the African-instituted churches on the continent. One of my most unusual journeys took me to the 'New Jerusalem', the Church's shrine at Nkamba, which in 1989 was a four-hour drive from Kinshasa. Kimbangu, brought up a Baptist, had a brief five-month ministry in and around Nkamba, begun on 6 April 1921. His activity displeased the Belgian authorities and he spent thirty years in prison in Lubumbashi in the south of Zaire, while his followers were deported by the thousand to concentration camps all over the country. The prophet died in 1951; the movement lived on and eventually, under a more liberal Belgian government, was allowed to become a church shortly before independence.

At its birth the church instantly had three million members and continued to grow. It was admitted to membership of the World Council of Churches in 1969, and its relationship with British Methodism originated with Bena Silu, a nuclear physicist who studied in Birmingham in the 1970s.

Bena Silu was in many ways the Kimbanguists' roving ambassador. Albert Mosley visited the Church in 1981 and my visit in turn was at the invitation of the Chef Spirituel, His Eminence Diangienda Kuntima. Diangienda was Simon Kimbangu's youngest son. Familiar with the story of Prophet Harris in Côte d'Ivoire, I was keen to discover the Kimbanguists for myself.

None the less I was nervous. Zaire was under the thumb of the dictator and kleptocrat General Mobutu (the name reverted to Democratic Republic of Congo when in 1997 he was overthrown after 32 years in power). For over two decades, in a drive for what he called 'authenticity', Zairians were forbidden to use Christian names and were enjoined to address each other as 'Citizen'. But I did not need to worry. I was extremely well received and cared for, both in Kinshasa and in Nkamba. From the airport I was taken to the luxurious guest house built for the visit of the Coptic pope Shenouda III and named after him; the manager at once phoned Nkamba to tell the Chef Spirituel I'd arrived, so that he could go to bed! Next door to the guest house a Conference Centre, equally lavish in conception, complete with interpreters' cabins and sub-committee rooms.

Kimbanguist headquarters Kinshasa.

The Kimbanguists had several large and lavish properties in the capital. In another quarter there was a four storey headquarters with offices and a computer training centre, run as a service by the church for its members. The Kimbanguist Hospital, on another site, had 200 beds, well-equipped theatres and an x-ray unit, a well-organized pharmacy and lab, with twelve doctors on the staff.

Sculpture at the Kimbanguist Hospital Kinshasa.

It was in a high-density, low-income area, built there to serve everybody. In yet another district, the great Kimbanguist temple – the French word for any place of worship, but best translated in this instance as 'cathedral' – seated six thousand. It had a balcony on three sides and in the middle of the fourth a fabulous dais with an ornate canopy, and plush armchairs for Kimbangu's three sons and for Mobutu should he be present. It was opened in 1966 – a remarkable achievement within seven years of the church emerging from clandestinity, especially in view of the chaos into which the country was plunged between 1960 and 1965.

But it is the general rule that Sunday worship takes place in the open air. I visited three congregations on Sunday morning, and the imposing temple itself was empty because the service was going on outside. It was difficult to estimate numbers because they were scattered in groups under each tree and other patches of shade, not massed together, and because many more were continuing to arrive at each of the prayer grounds as the service proceeded. Men and women sat in separate groups; the mixed choirs stood together to sing and then separated again. Exodus 3.5 was a golden rule and Kimbanguists go unshod in any place of prayer, inside or out.

I saw several primary and secondary schools. When the church was officially founded in 1959, and Kimbangu's followers in their hundreds of thousands left the mission churches where until then they had been members, their children were summarily expelled from the mission schools. Within weeks they were back in class in hastily organized Kimbanguist schools with voluntary teachers, many of them also dismissed by the missions. They ran the schools in this way for some years, until the government took responsibility for all teachers' salaries.

At the pump, Lutendele.

The High School in Kinshasa doubled as the School of Nursing in the afternoons – most school premises in the city were used by two different schools, am and pm.

I went out to the Kimbanguist Theological Faculty fifteen miles downstream, looking across the river (which was also known as the Zaire in those days) at the ex-French territory of Congo on the far side. I spent an hour talking with the 48 students and another hour with some of the 17 staff: an enviable ratio.

My escorts and I left Kinshasa in a battered Marina, loaded with plastic containers to bring back the treasured 'holy water' from the well at Nkamba. We took one of the country's main highways, yet for a long stretch progress was slow due to the poor state of repair. After 40 miles we transferred everything into a smart Pajero loaned, with driver, by a vice-minister in the government. Just as well, for when we turned off we were soon on steep, pitted, greasy roads.

The village of Nkamba, where Kimbangu was born and exercised his ministry and was arrested, and to which his remains were returned in 1960, is regarded as a holy place. Kimbanguists go barefoot, even at the end of the rainy season when the streets are rivers of mud. His Eminence the Chef Spirituel was at pains to indicate that this was not expected of me, nor was I to kneel when we conversed as every Kimbanguist automatically would.

At the centre of the village stood the massive temple, yet more imposing than the one in Kinshasa. With two levels of balconies, it would seat 37,000. The number was symbolic, for it was estimated that 37,000 families were deported during the period of persecution. Much of the village consisted of simple guest-houses, where the vast number of visitors could stay. A four-storey 'presidential' guest-house was nearly finished, with identical splendid apartments on each of three floors so that three heads of state could comfortably stay in Nkamba at the same time.

It was impossible to estimate the cost of all these properties. They were the fruit of amazing generosity. Many people contributed a third of their income. The craftsmen fitting out the guest-house were working simply for their keep. There were hundreds of people engaged daily in fetching stones by the bucketful from a quarry two kilometres away, or sitting outside the church manually breaking them, as their contribution to the ongoing construction.

Volunteer work-party preparing stones at Nkamba.

Among them were the leaders of the Kimbanguist movement in Congo and Angola, each humbly sharing in the manual work.

Diangienda gave me a cordial welcome. He was genuinely touched that I had come all that way, 'at such expense', to see him. He shared some of his concerns, particularly the feeling that Kimbanguism still had enemies. The years of persecution had left their mark, though there was no trace of rancour. Kimbangu's teaching was to render no evil for evil,

With His Eminence Joseph Diangienda Kuntima, Simon Kimbangu's youngest son.

112

and non-violence was a hallmark of the church. The Chef Spirituel was a clear thinker and a man of prayer, of warmth and openness. I gave him a copy of *Graines d'Evangile* ('Seeds of the Gospel'), a book I had edited about African-instituted Churches, and apologised that in it he is described as His Excellence not His Eminence! He took me into the mausoleum and led a prayer at the founder's tomb. On this occasion only, the prayer was addressed not to God, but to Kimbangu: Diangienda was talking to his father in the most natural way.

Outside again, there were speeches and a brass band and a final prayer before I climbed into the Pajero and was reunited with my shoes.

The Kimbanguists are a praying people. After every journey, thanks were offered for a safe arrival. Before every meal, sometimes before a bottle of soda, a prayer. Prayers were often in Lingala, the most widely-used of the four official vernaculars in Zaire, but I soon realised every prayer began and ended with the formula 'In the name of the Father and of the Son and of the Holy Spirit'. Greetings to a visitor were extended in the name of the Father – three claps – of the Son – three claps – and of the Holy Spirit – three claps.

I learned that baptism is, reflecting Kimbangu's Baptist origins, for believers, but that it is administered without water. Jesus, they explained, did not baptize with water, because he baptized with the Holy Spirit, and for Kimbanguist theology Jesus marked the end of the practice of water-baptism and the arrival of the era of Spirit-baptism: if God sends the Spirit on someone, surely water-baptism is unnecessary. However they recognized the validity of water-baptism practised in other churches and did not require rebaptism of those becoming Kimbanguists.

In spite of that oddity, it struck me that Kimbanguism and Methodism had much in common. Each has a charismatic founder (though Simon Kimbangu had a ministry of five months, John Wesley one of 53 years), a date to celebrate, a considerable impact on the history of the country. They each stress the ministry of the whole people of God, and have a keen sense of social justice. Kimbanguism's ecumenical theology echoes Wesley's, and its practice of the collective confessional resembles the early class-meetings. To live for a few days in the Kimbanguist world was to be puzzled and impressed, enriched and challenged.

CHAPTER 19

West Africa to West Indies

The initials MCOD stood for Methodist Church Overseas Division. I liked to say that they also stood for Multi-Cultural Omni-Directional: for Christian mission was no longer the one-way traffic of earlier times. Europe was on the receiving end of missionaries from churches which not so long ago had been 'mission fields'. Mission in reverse was a slogan some used to describe the trend. But omni-directional was more than that. Several ministers from the Caribbean had been stationed in The Gambia over recent years.

I devised a pilot scheme whereby ministers from Ghana would serve in the West Indies. They would be appointed by the Ghana Methodist Church. They would be stationed by the Methodist Church of the Caribbean and the Americas (MCCA), and while there would receive their stipend locally. But MCOD would facilitate the arrangement, providing the Ghanaians with a term's preparation at Kingsmead College in Selly Oak and paying their travel costs. As far as I remember, it would be a five or six-year appointment, but they would go on furlough to Ghana after three years, in the same way that British missionaries came home on furlough.

Ghana selected two ministers. Hayford Adu-Darkwa, a French speaker, went to Jérémie in Haiti, and Justice Dadson to the island of Grand Turk. A few months after they arrived I was able to visit them, because I was appointed to represent the British Conference at the 1990 Conference of the MCCA. En route to Nassau, where the Conference met, I spent a week in Jamaica, a week in Haiti and two days on Grand Turk.

Among the many folk I met in Jamaica were Philip Potter, Hugh Sherlock and Ivy McGhie. Philip, from the island of Dominica, was one of my mentors. He had been on the MMS staff in the 1960s and went on to be the General Secretary of the World Council of Churches, based in Geneva; now in retirement he was back in the Caribbean for a few years.

Hugh, who had been the first President of the MCCA, was the author of the Jamaican national anthem – composed in a day, he told me, while changing planes in Bogota. He took me in his old banger to Boys' Town, a centre he'd started in 1940. As we drove through West Kingston he told me this area was in his mind when he wrote the words of his hymn, 'In the streets of every city where the bruised and lonely dwell'.

Philip Potter in retirement.

Ivy was a colleague at MCOD and had been one of the facilitators at the consultations in Ghana and Nigeria. She gave me three bags of Blue Mountain coffee as gifts for friends in England. No sooner did I arrive in Haiti than one was slit open by a zealous customs official to check it contained coffee not drugs.

After a busy day or two in and around Port-au-Prince, I was to fly down to Jérémie. My host was in no hurry to get me to the airport and we arrived with only a few minutes to spare. It was a domestic flight so there were few formalities, but I had not yet bought my ticket! "I think I'd better drop you off at the terminal door – the ticket counter is immediately on the left," explained Edouard.

"A single to Jérémie," I asked at the counter. "Name?" "Pritchard." I handed over my $45 and was shown where to sit. Then I was approached by someone who asked, "Jérémie?" and picked up my bag. Walking off, he looked over his shoulder and said, "Come on." So I followed him out to the plane, climbed in after my bag, and suddenly realised that my name was the only one on the list they had checked at the counter! What's more, the baggage-handler was the pilot. As we taxied down the runway, I said to him, "I hope you're feeling well today …"

We flew down the gulf. From the air it was plain to see how much silt was being washed away where rivers drained into the sea, brown stains on the blue. Deforestation was taking its toll.

The short drive into Jérémie from the airstrip felt very African: a mixture of stone houses, wood houses, houses of mud and houses of corrugated-iron sheeting. The street through the centre of town was tarred. The Methodist compound was up the hill, with a good view from the Adu-Darkwas' veranda. The Jérémie circuit super, Moïse, lived next door. He rejoiced that he now had a colleague to share the care of 37 churches and another dozen outposts. Both he and Hayford were guarded in what they said, both when we were all together and in private discussions, but I sensed that relationships would not be easy. In fact for various reasons the appointment didn't work out and the family left much sooner than planned.

Hayford Adu-Darkwa in Jérémie.

After a weekend of conversations, meetings, services and visits, Hayford drove me back to the capital. The first three hours through the mountains to Les Cayes were breath-taking.

I noted in my journal: 'The road may be much improved, with only a couple of fords and plenty of bridges, but it is rougher and far more spectacular than the Bandiagara road in Mali.' The road north to Cap Haitien, a couple of days later, was amazing too. I was driven by Chenet Paul, the Cap Haitien minister. In a five hours journey we started out along the coast, traversed rice plains, passed through a desert region where cactus proliferated but an irrigation project had created a banana grove, continued up a fertile valley with mangoes and orchards, and eventually took a mountain road to the coast. Once we passed the col, at a place delightfully named

Marmelade, where it was distinctly chilly, the terrain on the descent became noticeably more wooded; deforestation had left its ugly mark all the way up.

From Cap Haitien I flew to Grand Turk. At the airport my baggage proved overweight and they refused to check me in. I hung around, thinking they might relent, but to no avail. In the end I had to extract some of my gear from the suitcase and stuff it into my hand luggage. This made no difference to the total weight I took on board, but satisfied the red tape.

It was another six-seater, but this time every seat was full. We were cramped, but only for 45 minutes. Justice Dadson was waiting to greet me. He had settled in well, although the family were still in a rented house while the new circuit manse was being finished.

Justice Dadson in Grand Turk.

The Turks and Caicos Islands are a British Overseas Territory with a population, at that time, of about 15,000; 5,000 lived on Grand Turk, an island measuring three miles by five miles. The Methodist circuit consisted of five churches on five of the seven inhabited islands; Justice flew off every weekend except the first of the month.

Cockburn Town, the capital of Turks and Caicos since 1766, is on Grand Turk. Justice was already well known and took me to meet many folk, beginning with the Governor. He explained the division of responsibilities between himself as a London appointee and the elected Chief Minister of the territory. He bemoaned the shortage of person-power to do all he'd like to see done to develop the islands, since 30,000 islanders lived outside the territory. There were acres of derelict salt pans; the salt industry died in the 1940s. Tourism on the island of Providenciales (known as Provo) was the biggest income generator and now had the largest population.

Grand Turk was a peaceful backwater (though perhaps that's not an apt word, since one was always within sound and generally within sight of the sea). The Dadsons happily went out leaving the children alone in the house for a short while, with the front door open. I found it most reassuring. When I left, it was on a plane with two pilots and two passengers – the other was the Speaker of the Turks and Caicos Parliament. We called at Provo and picked up more passengers, and flew on to Nassau.

The Methodist Conference included people from all over the Caribbean, Guyana, Panama and Belize; apart from the Bahamians, I was the only one who had not travelled via Miami. Mine was the more picturesque journey.

Home from home? Nassau, Bahamas
with Clare Holder, organiser of the Notting Hill Carnival.

This is not the place to relate the proceedings of the Conference nor the tensions that would soon split Methodism in the Bahamas. I was briefly transported back to Africa when I discovered the 'Ivory Coast' Seafood and Steak restaurant. I found time to swim in the sea off every island I visited on the trip, but here it was not the Caribbean, but the Atlantic.

Flying back to England, we touched down in Bermuda – another of those places I have 'been to' but never got beyond the airport.

As there was nothing else to do in the transit lounge I got on with a book I was reading, *The Bible in the Modern World*. Imagine my surprise when I turned a page and read 'Harry was born in Bermuda, so, presumably, Harry is a British subject, since a man born in Bermuda will generally be a British subject'. The reason for this instance of logic is immaterial. The fact is, I know of no other reference to Bermuda in any work of theology, and I chanced to read it on the spot.

CHAPTER 20

Freedom is Coming

The former German colony of South West Africa fell under South African control after the First World War. Although at first the League of Nations and later the United Nations officially exercised oversight of the mandate, South Africa refused to acknowledge their role or to contemplate independence for the territory. In 1966 the UN General Assembly declared the mandate terminated and in 1971 the International Court of Justice ruled that South Africa's presence there was illegal. In 1968 a UN resolution changed South West Africa's name to Namibia, though the main Namibian independence movement was still the South West Africa People's Organisation (SWAPO).

Ninety per cent of Namibia's population is Christian and in 1978 Anglicans, Lutherans, Roman Catholics and the small Methodist District formed the Council of Churches. Its role was to speak with a united voice against injustice on behalf of the voiceless; and to initiate relief projects for the poor. In solidarity with them the British Council of Churches set up a Namibia Group, which at one stage I chaired. I was at a meeting with Bernt Carlsson, the UN Commissioner for Namibia, just a couple of days before he died on Pan Am Flight 103, which was sabotaged over Lockerbie in December 1988.

Independence would not be denied. UN Security Council resolution 435 had been passed back in 1978. It called for a ceasefire and for UN-supervised elections. South Africa finally agreed to implement it on the day after Carlsson died and the elections for a Constituent Assembly were held in November 1989. It emerged later that the South African government paid more than £20 million to at least seven political parties in Namibia to oppose SWAPO. A large international corps of observers went to monitor the election campaign and the vote; I was one.

I travelled via Harare where, as well as doing business, I spent some time with my daughter Claire. She had graduated in the summer and was spending a few months helping at a Children's Home.

Then I continued to Cape Town for the MCSA Conference. It met in the Clifford Storey Hall: a name familiar to me not only because his son Peter had greeted me on my first arrival in South Africa in 1987, but also because it is inscribed on a board in what is now known as the Richmond Room at Methodist Church House in London. It is almost the last entry on a series of boards that came from Richmond College when it closed; they list those students who went overseas between 1844 and 1938.

On my immigration form I had said that I was 'visiting friends' and in the Conference I was surrounded by them. Things were moving in South Africa. The next morning came news that Walter Sisulu and seven other political prisoners were released at dawn. Stanley Mogoba, the President of the Conference and a one-time companion of Mandela's on Robben Island, told me that the last time he'd been to see Nelson in prison he was able to overstay the 45 minutes he'd been allocated.

The possibility of Mandela's release was being mooted, and with hindsight it is clear that some people knew more than they were prepared to say. I noted in my journal, 'He will only agree to come out when a negotiating structure has been agreed – it sounds as though he's calling the tune'. As indeed he was. The song 'Freedom is coming, yes I know' was being sung with ever increasing confidence. It came first in Namibia.

I would cover five thousand miles in the next three weeks, mostly at the wheel myself, but initially, on the long drive from Cape Town to Windhoek, with Jimmy Palos. We again took the detour to Finger Rock which had collapsed in December 1988, the pillar probably weakened by a rare rainstorm and finished off by a tremor from a distant earthquake. Jimmy enlivened the journey with quips such as 'What kind of music do you like?' – 'Both kinds; Country *and* Western', and the candidate for the ministry who was asked, "What is your most besetting sin?" and replied, "Giving impudent answers to impudent questions!"

The first night we stopped at a motel and the second at a conference centre for a Local Preachers' convention, which was all in Afrikaans. We got to Windhoek on Saturday evening, in time for me to preach next morning.

Electioneering was in full flow. The Churches Information and Monitoring Service was at the centre of a complex and ever-changing logistical operation: booking hotels and guest-houses, hiring vehicles and planes, meeting flights on which people did not arrive …

Voter education.

It was managed by a Briton, Sarah Hayward, who was funded by the BCC Namibia Group that I chaired. She was inordinately busy, but eventually – when all the international observers had been dispatched to the far-flung corners of the land, we had supper together and she poured out her frustrations.

By that time the election itself, a five-day operation, was under way. Before that, I'd shared in ten days of monitoring. The verb 'to monitor' had well and truly entered the Namibian vocabulary. As in the quip: 'I love work; I could monitor it all day'! A parent asks a teenager 'Where are you going?' and the reply is 'I'm going monitoring.' There are those who *do* and those who *monitor*.

My base was a basement: a small studio flat below the Windhoek manse, which had an unpleasant smell to it that I never tracked down. But I was always out and about, looking out for trouble or intimidation at party rallies, meeting polling station chiefs, hearing stories, rumours, hopes and fears from black, white and 'coloured' people, as well as attending services, preaching and discussing Methodist matters with my hosts. Communications difficulties did not always allow me to make all the contacts I had planned, but I generally made others. I was able to get journalist accreditation, which proved useful on occasion. I put myself down as Africa Correspondent of the *Methodist Recorder* – I could probably have claimed *The Times* or the *Jewish Chronicle* with impunity, as my card was ready before I finished completing the three-page application form.

I drove down to the coast in a hire car and had two nights in Walvis Bay, a South African enclave, with border formalities to complete. The last stretch of road ran between the sea and the desert. At one point a road sign bore the legend 'Sand', which was rather stating the obvious!

There was an empty church flat I could use, for there was no longer a minister; there were too few members to support one, since most of the white members had left a Church which supported Namibian independence. The main election issue was to ensure that 10,500 registered Namibian voters could get to the nearest polling station in Swakopmund along the coast.

I spent an interesting morning at Narraville High School, where the principal was a Methodist. It was well equipped, but struggled to keep the desert at bay. The grass was scorched by encroaching sand, and the boundary fence seemed likely to collapse under its weight. I met with the staff at their mid-morning break and was treated to a fashion parade by girls displaying their needlework.

Fashion parade Narraville High School.

The school was managed, under the segregated South African system, by the Department of Coloured Education, and the nearest similar school was hundreds of miles away, so one anxiety was about sports competitions. They'd been assured that, since SWAPO considered Walvis Bay to be Namibian anyway, there'd be no problem. (The enclave was transferred to Namibia in 1994 by the new South African government.)

Diaz cross, near Luderitz.

I got back to Windhoek, a 170 mile drive, on Friday lunchtime and was at once whisked off to Keetmanshoop, 300 miles south. From there, with a local evangelist for company, I drove on Saturday morning to the fishing port of Luderitz. We passed ostriches and springbok, as the farmlands gave way to desert. In spite of a puncture we arrived in plenty of time for the SWAPO rally and while my companion went off to conduct a funeral I took the chance to visit Diaz Point, where the Portuguese navigator Bartolomeo Diaz had erected a cross in 1488.

The dirt road passed through a desolate moonscape dotted with ghost houses from abandoned diamond workings.

Kolmanskop ghost town near Luderitz

At Diaz Point there was one car parked and as I made my way to the cross – a modern replacement – I met a couple of Yorkshiremen lurching back through the wind over the footbridge. "'Ang on to yer glasses," I was warned. The wind blew at gale force and I did not linger. Back at the carpark, my fellow tourists had gone and the ignition wouldn't come on. I decided not to panic and enjoyed a sandwich and a juice. Some people testify that in a like quandary they fall to prayer. My lunch worked just as well. For some reason the car now started first time, but I didn't dare switch the engine off again until I was safely back in Luderitz!

The sports field was awash with SWAPO flags and the crowd wore an assortment of t-shirts, cloths, scarves and pullovers all in blue, red and green. There were five vehicles from UNTAG (the United Nations Transition Assistance Group) keeping an eye on proceedings. The main speaker referred to the fact that there were very few whites at the rally – actually I think I was the only one.

A display followed, by about fifty children in SWAPO colours, who must have rehearsed their complex routine at length. I was able to talk to a number of people in the crowd.

Next day I preached in Luderitz, with Afrikaans-interpretation, and after lunch drove back to Keetmanshoop, just in time, despite another puncture and a swift wheel change, for the 6 pm service.

"I told you you'd puncture if you did more than 50kph on the grit road," said Ralph, the minister who'd lent the car. Well, he was right; but I think those tyres would have punctured at any speed.

It is over 500 miles from Windhoek to Ruacana on the Angolan border. The Ruacana Falls, one of the largest waterfalls in Africa, were not our destination, but Simon Heim, my

Simon Heim (in Ovamboland).

companion on a journey to the north, and I went to have a look one day when the planned programme went awry.

Ruacana Falls dry due to diversion of the water to the hydroelectric station.

As it turned out, they were dry: when the Cunene river is low, all the water is channelled through the hidden turbines of the hydroelectric power station.

The BP filling station attendant was wearing a SWAPO badge, but he said, "You don't know what's in my mind." The message had got through; 'Vote Without Fear' and 'Your Vote is Your Secret' were placarded in several languages everywhere.

We drove alongside an irrigation canal which, mile after mile, provided a focal point for the community life of humans and beasts alike.

Irrigation canal, Ovamboland.

Back in Oshikuku we met the election director for the region. She was worried whether there would be enough time for everyone to vote – Ovamboland was the most populous area of the country outside the capital, and the 'voter education' meetings she'd organised were crowded. There were 357 polling stations for the whole of Namibia: 226 were static for the five days, together with 131 mobile stations, some of which were scheduled to visit as many as five different places in the course of a single day. A handful of extra stations was added to the list at the last moment, but information about the venues was not easily available until it was published in the press on the first day of voting.

After three days in the north, we got back to Windhoek in time for a briefing for the 'Eminent Persons' who had arrived to witness the five day election. Jimmy Palos gave a prayerful and then a passionate start to the proceedings. Afterwards they were despatched in ten teams around the country.

I stayed in Windhoek for the first two days of polling before flying home. They were without doubt the most memorable days of all the five years I spent as Africa Secretary. It was nothing like any election Britain has ever seen.

This is an edited version of what I wrote on the afternoon of Day 1:

'At Goreangab Primary School several hundred voters were waiting patiently for the polling station to open as 7 am arrived. The minutes passed. Inside, the election officials, UNTAG representatives and observers from seven of the ten parties contesting the election were painstakingly verifying that the ballot boxes were properly sealed.

At 7.23 the queue began to move, as four of the Namibian officials checked fingers under the ultra-violet scanner to ensure no-one had voted already, checked that the registration card and the photo-identity card carried the same details, confirmed that the registration number was not on the list of numbers requiring double-checking, then moistened the voter's fingers with invisible but indelible ink, tore out the first ballot paper from the first book, stamped the reverse with the official stamp, and at last – into the polling booth, cast your vote, come out and post the folded ballot paper, showing the official stamp to the UNTAG monitor, into the ballot box.

The whole procedure took about three minutes per voter.

First to cast their votes were a couple called Issakar and Susanna, who had been waiting since around 5 am.

They were followed by Harold Urib, a doctoral student in political science in Paris, who returned to Namibia in July and will return to France to pursue his studies later this month. Hesitatingly this political scientist enquired, "Is it all right to wear party symbols?"

Apart from a handful of red and white DTA caps there were no other signs of party allegiance in the queue. But Harold decided to open his waistcoat and reveal the SWAPO T-shirt underneath.'

Shortly afterwards senior UNTAG officials visited the polling station. I asked if, because of the late start, the station would stay open later in the evening, and was assured that all those still queuing at 7 pm would be allowed to cast their votes. At two nearby stations queues were much longer. Some foresighted people brought seats.

7am, queuing to vote.

As the morning wore on party symbols became more evident – particularly the SWAPO umbrellas to afford protection from the blinding sun. To witness the good humour, discipline, incredible patience and determination of these vast crowds was a very moving experience.

Queuing in the sun.

It seemed as though everybody wanted to vote at the earliest opportunity, but just across the road, workers in blue overalls were busy laying new kerbstones. One was carefully pointing out the taut string to passers-by. "What day are you going to vote?" I asked him. "SWAPO," he replied.

In some places voters were advised at noon that the length of the queue gave them no chance of voting that day and they dispersed peacefully.

By the second day voting was more brisk as the officials became more practised and voters knew what to expect. In those two days I visited eight of the thirteen stations in Windhoek and noted nothing amiss. Country-wide the elections were judged 'free and fair', even if some found them 'free and frustrating'.

Midday queuing to vote.

The result gave SWAPO a majority in the Constituent Assembly, though not the two-thirds majority it hoped for, and Namibia became independent in March 1990.

If the Namibian people were making history, history was made in the eyes of the world that February when Nelson Mandela was released. I was deep in the Sierra Leone bush when he walked out of Pollsmoor prison, but the BBC World Service brought me the news. My pocket-size shortwave radio accompanied me on all my travels.

When I got home I found that Claire, now back from Zimbabwe, had recorded for me five hours of television coverage of that momentous day, which I devoured.

Freedom was coming in South Africa too. But as it turned out I never returned to South Africa. By the time 'One Person One Vote' became a reality there, I had become General Secretary of the Overseas Division, with different responsibilities.

CHAPTER 21

Emancipation and Enfranchisement

'World Village' was an annual convention organized by the Overseas Division. In planning the 1994 event, we bore in mind that it would coincide with the 160th anniversary of the abolition of slavery in British territories. That prompted me, early in the year, to write an article which the *Methodist Recorder* published with the title 'Freedom and Prayer'.

I wrote:

'What have 27 April 1994 and 1 August 1834 in common? Quite a lot. 1 August 1834 was Emancipation Day: 160 years ago slavery was abolished 'throughout the British colonies, plantations and possessions abroad'. Decades of struggle and campaigning finally attained their objective. 27 April this year is election day in South Africa: Stanley Mogoba, Nelson Mandela, Desmond Tutu and millions of others will cast their votes for the first time in their lives.

Decades of resistance to apartheid have at last achieved the enfranchisement of South Africa's black people – something for which we have hoped and prayed, yet scarcely dared to believe we would ever see. What Emancipation Day was, especially in the West Indies, election day is in South Africa.

In both cases we are talking as much about a beginning as an end. The lives of the slaves did not change out of all recognition overnight. Indeed the Abolition Act provided that slaves should remain in the service of their present masters for another four years as 'free apprenticed labourers, under agreed conditions of labour', which appeared to them to be taking back with the left hand what it conferred with the right. Slavery they knew well; freedom they understood and looked for; but apprenticeship was neither one thing nor the other.

The arrangement worked with varying success from island to island. In Antigua it was judged unnecessary and the slaves obtained immediate unqualified freedom. On the small islands there was often sufficient cooperation to see the transitional phase through, though emancipation never meant anything remotely approaching equal rights. On the great estates belonging to absentee owners, especially in Jamaica, the apprentices found themselves cheated and abused, victims of unscrupulous managers who had not given up their slave-driving habits. They worked sullenly and deserted the plantation at the first opportunity. Substitute labour was not to be had, and many a sugar estate soon ceased production and reverted to scrub.

It is clear that the lives of black South Africans will not be transformed overnight either. Homelessness and unemployment on a massive scale will not be eradicated. One of the fears for the future is that people will expect more of the first government they have ever voted for than any government can possibly deliver. Real change – economic empowerment and opportunity, education of quality for all – is only just beginning. But that takes nothing from the historic moment that 27 April will be. I had the never-to-be-forgotten privilege of observing Namibia's first election in 1989, when mile-long queues of voters waited patiently, good-humouredly beneath a blazing sun to exercise their vote, while South African and UN police looked on benignly. Namibia's development as an independent nation still proceeds slowly, but that was the turning point. This year it is South Africa's turn at last.

A third similarity between 1834 and 1994 is the involvement of the Churches and Christian leaders in paving the way. Both in Britain and the Caribbean, Christians were at the forefront of the anti-slavery movement. Many a Methodist missionary suffered at the hands of slave-owners for his outspokenness; many of the slaves who played a leading part in manifestations of discontent were Methodist preachers. Slaves were brutally punished and many paid with their lives; in smaller numbers, white folk who took their part were run off the islands, their houses ransacked or torched. The involvement of Christians, black and white, both inside and outside South Africa, in the anti-apartheid struggle is just as noteworthy. The names of Tutu and Huddleston may be the best-known, but the list is so long that it would fill several disks of the South African Justice Department computer.

A call to prayer is being issued to the British Churches to mark Enfranchisement Day. It could be a day of unprecedented violence and bloodshed ... I hope it will rather be the experience of Namibia on a grand scale. One reason for confidence is the extent of the monitoring operations that are being put in place by the United Nations and other bodies, including the ecumenical programme linked with the South African Council of Churches in which a number of British Methodists are taking part. Another reason is the great outpouring of prayer worldwide that will seal all the praying for South Africa we have done for many years ...

On 31 July 1834 Methodist congregations throughout the Caribbean gathered for watchnight services. In packed churches, as midnight struck, those slaves received their freedom on their knees in prayer, not out on the street getting drunk and rioting. Watchnight services are a distinctive Methodist tradition; and I suggest that the distinctive Methodist response to the call to prayer for South Africa in April should take the form of watchnight services in every circuit ...

It will be a time to give God thanks for so many sacrifices in the cause of freedom and justice, to remember the martyrs who longed to see this day, and to pray that peaceful, free and fair elections may mark the beginning of a new and wholesome stage in Africa's history.'

I do not know how many such services were held. God alone knows how many prayers were said. The world knows that the election brought a black majority government to power, and Mandela became the first President of a free South Africa.

CHAPTER 22

Leisure Time

On two occasions I was able to combine a work assignment with some time off. Pat did not normally travel with me, as she had her job at Mount Vernon Hospital, but she came with me to The Gambia once. It was the nearest port of call on my Africa round (and therefore the cheapest flight!). There'd been a Methodist Church in The Gambia since 1821, but it was still small.

John Stedman, who had welcomed us in Ghana after our tour of the Sahel, had since moved to Banjul and, with the retirement of Ernest Stafford, one of the rare Gambian District Chairmen in history, had been asked to take over. In September 1989 I went out to induct him into office. I had been there in January for the District Synod and done the essential business, so apart from the service it would be a relaxing week. Indeed it was, when we got there – after the panic was over.

We were flying on Tuesday so I was making ready at the weekend, when to my horror I discovered that Pat's passport was out of date. In fact it had expired twelve months previously while we were in France, and she had travelled home without a valid passport – which no border control had picked up. So by 7 am on Monday I was standing in a long queue at the Passport Office in Westminster, waiting for it to open at 9. It was 10 by the time I reached a desk, but with the tickets to demonstrate the urgency of my application I was told to return at 3 and collect a new one. It was a short day at the office, but we flew as planned. (A more serious lapse occurred in 1994 when I arrived in Belize and discovered I'd left my ticket on the plane from Miami. It was Labor Day in America and there was no chance of recovering it. But I phoned the office in London and a duplicate was wired through – it helped that Verna Anderson who handled MCOD travel arrangements was herself a Belizean!)

Earlier in the year John had baptized the baby of the manager

Pat at Marakissa clinic.

of the Atlantic Hotel – and in gratitude he let us have a room at a cut-price rate. We made the most of it: wonderful al fresco buffet breakfasts, daily use of the pool, a tie-dye lesson for Pat, sunburn for me after I spent too long talking church matters with John when I emerged from my first swim!

I took Pat to see the agricultural project at Brikama and the clinic at Marakissa.

On Sunday I duly inducted John and the holiday was over all too soon.

A more energetic few days off: in January 1992 I climbed Mount Kenya.

By then I had suddenly found myself Acting General Secretary of the Overseas Division, when my predecessor resigned.

I took the helm at a time of financial crisis. There was every reason to stay at my desk. But the Kenyan Church (MCK) was long overdue for a visit and, although I had contrived to appoint a temporary part-time Acting Africa Secretary, it was on the understanding he would not be undertaking any overseas travel.

So I made just the one exception that year to my desk-bound rule, and managed to tag four days on at the end for a mountaineering expedition. It was a very full three weeks. It included a drive to Mwanza, at the southern end of Lake Victoria, stopping en route to see a handful of Tanzanian congregations that MCK had taken under its wing.

On the way back to Nairobi, late at night, driving up the Rift Valley from Nakuru, a zebra sauntered into our path, and only some very deft manoeuvring prevented us tumbling down the escarpment – that's a zebra crossing I never want to see again!

A flight to Mombasa, with a stunning view of Kilimanjaro most of the way; a drive to Lamu Island, stopping at the remote hospital at Ngao and at the church in Golbanti with the graves of John and Annie Houghton, who were murdered by Maasai in 1886; we reached the jetty at Mokowe after the last scheduled ferry to Lamu had left, stood and watched the sun set, and succeeded in getting a dhow to take us across. Later on, the night train from Mombasa to Nairobi, chugging uphill at an average of 23 mph and arriving exactly on time; a meeting of an 'African Methodist Summit' with bishops from across the continent, chaired by my old friend Sunday Mbang from Nigeria. After all that I was ready for a breather … if climbing to 4985m (16,354ft) can be so called.

At the start of my visit I had been to Maua hospital. John Harbottle, the medical superintendent, and his wife Sharon had planned the expedition and I was joining them.

We met up at Kaaga, where the Methodist Theological Institute has in more recent times expanded into a Methodist University. We drove up to 3,017m and walked for a couple of hours, getting used to the altitude. We spent the first night in a lodge and then drove to 3,150m where we shouldered our backpacks and began walking at 8.45 pm.

Austrian hut and glacier, below Point Lenana.

As we climbed we were soon surrounded by the unusual vegetation of the area: the terrain sprouts several species of giant plants: groundsel, thistle and lobelia. By 4 pm we reached Mintos Hut at 4,300m, where we spent a long, cold night in the company of two French girls and their guide, the six of us ranged along a shelf on one side of the tin shelter. It was sub-zero outside but I was warm enough in long johns and socks, four layers of upper garments, a woolly hat and a sleeping bag, all (or most) kindly loaned by the Harbottles.

Next morning we headed for the summit, taking just one pack with food and emergency equipment. We reckoned it was safe to leave the rest of our gear at Mintos. We set off at 8.15 and reached the Austrian Hut (4,790m) in four hours. We left our kit there and headed for the glacier – just another 200m of ascent to the top. Point Lenana is only the third highest summit in the massif, but like most trekkers who declare they have 'climbed Mt Kenya' Lenana was our goal. We struggled up through cloud, which kindly parted for a few minutes when we got there. We made it back to Mintos by 5.30 pm.

The hut was crowded that night. There were seven Europeans on the shelf and a dozen porters on the floor below. Two of them left at 2 am to take a party who were camping nearby to see the sun rise at the summit. I slept no more and was outside well before dawn, gazing eastwards into the darkness waiting for the first light of day. The wait was cold but could not cool my exhilaration. The sun appeared on the dot of 6.30. After that it was downhill all the way.

Egypt was not on my work schedule. When we went in 1996 it was

Abu Simbel.

for a holiday. We had a few days in Cairo: the Egyptian Museum, the pyramids of Giza and an excursion to Memphis and Saqqara.

We flew to Abu Simbel and marvelled not only at the colossal statues of Ramses II, but the extraordinary engineering feat which had moved it before it could sink beneath the rising waters of Lake Nasser and had replaced it, 90 metres above its original level, exactly where twice a year the light of the rising sun falls on the gods sitting in the shrine as it did two millennia previously.

We cruised down the Nile from Aswan to Luxor, and here misfortune befell us. Our party made an early start for the Valley of the Kings. But first we stopped at a small (how small I'll never know) tomb in the Valley of the Queens. For the first time in the week we needed the powerful torch we'd been told to bring, to see the wall decorations as we made our way to the first chamber.

Pat was just in front of me, shining the light on the wall. As the Arab attendant turned away to ask for baksheesh from the couple before us, she took a step to the right – and disappeared with a scream. For all I knew, that hole of darkness was thirty metres deep. In fact it was only three – enough to do permanent damage to her arm, and leave her head to be stitched without anaesthetic in the primitive west bank hospital.

Once stitched up, we were whisked back across the Nile to Luxor hospital to set the arm in plaster. No more sightseeing. But she survived. After a painful, sleepless night on the ship we flew to Cairo and fell so sound asleep in the hotel that we knew nothing of an earthquake that afternoon, epicentred on Cyprus, that shook the city. We have had no more African holidays.

CHAPTER 23

Uganda
Community Development through Sport

In 2002 my brother Colin, a keen mountaineer, went climbing in the Rwenzori mountains, Uganda, labelled long ago by Ptolemy 'the Mountains of the Moon'. It was there he got to know Augustine Muhindo, who started the Rwenzori Parents' Primary School for Orphans and Needy in Ibanda, a large village in the foothills. The people of the region live on the poverty line. Few homes have running water, electricity or basic sanitation and jobs are scarce. Out of his contact with Augustine arose a novel project, working with young people to help build their self-esteem and self-respect.

It so happened that Colin's son, Stephen, was at a loose end and was persuaded to help kick-start the project: an appropriate metaphor for two reasons. Firstly because the core activities at the outset were football and netball – and Stephen is never happier than when he has a ball to kick. Secondly because transport around the area relies on boda-bodas, Uganda's ubiquitous motorbike taxis.

Stephen arrived in 2007 to join two full-time Ugandan staff, who got £3 per week. CDTS was soon working in 17 schools each week and in the evenings at five village pitches. At weekends there were training sessions for referees and for coaches.

CDTS football team.

As time went by and finances allowed, more staff joined the team. One young man spent his full time repairing balls to keep them in play. The number of schools involved rose to 36 and in school holidays coaching sessions and matches were organized in 25 villages. The staff used boda-bodas to move around the region. CDTS arranged tournaments for different age groups, and entered its 'spearhead' teams in regional competitions.

Some financial support came from the local hydropower company. Stephen, a fan of Glasgow Celtic, got the Celtic Charity Fund to supply kit for the CDTS team; when it arrived, in Colin's baggage, most strips turned out to be XL in size, and the local people tend to be small in stature, but they wore it with pride and earned promotion! Links were also established for a while with the Hampshire F.A. Community Trust, who shipped a quantity of new and used equipment via Mombasa. Customs and overland transport issues made for long delays, extra costs and loss of hair before it finally reached Ibanda.

I was talking about the venture with one of my neighbours, who told me about KitAid. KitAid is a charity that recycles football strips to some of the world's poorest countries. I was able to collect four large cartons from one of its depots in a Sussex barn, packed with a dozen complete sets of shirts recycled from clubs large and small, shorts, socks, goalies' gloves and more.

At that point CDTS was expecting a visit from Solent University students, at the prompting of Hants F.A. They would take it out in their accompanied baggage, as Colin had taken the Celtic kit, saving all the hassle of the previous shipment. In the event the students' visit was postponed, then cancelled, and the cartons spent a couple of years in our garage. In 2013 I decided to do something about it.

In January I had visited Cuba with a group from the Christians Aware organization. Because I was now over 70, I found getting travel insurance quite costly; in fact the best quote I got was for an annual policy. And since I had an annual policy, why not make another trip? By this time Stephen had a partner and a baby in Ibanda.

Although the project management was now in Ugandan hands, Stephen was staying put – and hoping to land a coaching job with one of the country's premier teams. So Colin was going to Ibanda again in June, prior to a meeting in Kenya he was involved in. We arranged to meet in Amsterdam and travel together, and Paul (my son) agreed to come with us.

Paul runs a removal firm and he had the job of squeezing the contents of four cartons into three 20 kg bags of the dimensions KLM would accept. His professional expertise did the trick. When we booked the flight with KLM, the baggage allowance was two items of up to 20 kg each, which meant we could take one case for our personal effects and three bags for the kit; KLM subsequently reduced the allowance to one item each, but we had booked just in time.

Over the years Colin has got to know a delightful taxi-driver called Masaba, who met us at Entebbe airport when we emerged from customs at 11.15 pm into the hustle and bustle that were a far cry from my previous time there, in the lonely transit lounge at dead of night. He drove us to the Anglican Guest House on Namirembe hill, below St Paul's Cathedral.

We were not there for long. First thing next morning, down into traffic-clogged Kampala to change money before we set out on the long journey to Fort Portal. I wondered how long it had taken the British troops who built the original fort in 1891 to get there, presumably following the old Arab slave-routes. Later I learned that the Italian Duke of Abruzzi, whose expedition made first ascents of all sixteen summits in the Rwenzori range in 1906, took twenty-seven days from Entebbe, marching with 300 porters!

The surfaced road was good, but at every town and village there was a series of traffic-calming measure: pronounced rumble strips and obese 'sleeping policemen' at frequent intervals until the buildings gave way to banana groves, maize fields, tea or sugar plantations. There was good reason for them, as we realised when a bus came hurtling past us on a bend. They have doubtless saved many lives. But they not only slow the journey, they must increase fuel consumption considerably.

After lunch and tea stops, it was almost dusk when we reached Ibanda. Once three separate villages, it straggled for a couple of miles up the road. We were struck by the numbers of children – older ones just out of classroom after a long school day, younger ones playing with their simple homemade toys, lots of curiosity as we climbed out of the car to stretch our cramped limbs.

Traders were doing business. There was a queue of youngsters outside a shop advertising 'Hair Shaving Battery and Phone Charging', but it transpired they were waiting to watch television, for there was a satellite dish nearby. Uganda's hills boasted plenty of relay masts; cellphone signals were easy to pick up.

We met the family at the CDTS office and then checked in at the grandly named Rwenzori Base Camp Holiday Inn. By the time we got back to the office for breakfast next morning, the kit had been unpacked and most of it stacked away.

There was no hand-over ceremony. Janet Kaminyerie, the new project manager, judged it wise not to publicize its arrival far and wide. Things went missing all too easily. But soon local teams would be playing in Reading or Burnley shirts, or maybe Fittleworth or Curley Park Rangers.

Stephen and Annet had arranged the baptism of baby Matthew while we were there. That first morning we met with the local minister to plan the service, and the next day it took place. I preached; the baptism itself was performed by Alice Nobiye, chaplain at the Rwenzori High School. The school had 1,500 students. The colour of their trousers or skirts denoted their year. The school choir sang some lively choreographed songs in the service, taking their cue from the vivacious Alice. She also translated my message into Lukonjo. Once again I found myself wishing I'd kept count of the languages into which my sermons have been interpreted over the years.

After just three nights in Ibanda we were to make an early start on the long journey back to Kampala. But, before we were even loaded, the car, creeping past a truck unloading timber, hit a rock on the rutted and potholed village street. Masaba got us back down the valley to the tarred road, where the exhaust was repaired – a long job with lots of welding. Once again it was dark when we reached Kampala. Next morning Colin left for Mombasa, and Masaba took Paul and me on a tour of the city: the Buganda parliament building, the Kabaka's palace, the royal burial grounds, the Ba'hai temple. He took us out to Namugongo and the shrines of 22 Catholic and 23 Anglican martyrs, executed between November 1885 and January 1887. Then we drove along the busy road towards Kenya, through sugar plantations and a protected primal forest, across the Nile at the Owen Falls Dam and into Jinja.

Everywhere else in Uganda was new to me, but I had come overland as far as Jinja in 1988. There were a few Methodist congregations in the area and the Kenya Conference had taken them under its wing. There was one Ugandan probationer minister, Solomon Muwanga, who was a convert from Islam and had studied in the USA; later I ordained him back in Nairobi.

(The ordination could not be in Uganda as Solomon would have been responsible for all the arrangements, including hospitality for the many who would have wanted to come from Kenya; that would have distracted him from the purpose of the occasion.) Back then I had crossed the border crossing at Busia, where there was half a mile between the gates. People using public transport had to make their own way. This was where men with bicycles or motorbikes would wait to take them across the no man's land between the posts, and would shout to potential customers 'border-border': the origin of the name boda-boda.

On this occasion there was no church business. Paul and I spent our last night – my last night in Africa – at the Sunset Hotel and watched the sun go down over the Nile. In the morning we

Where the Nile leaves Lake Victoria.

took a three hour trip in a small boat on Lake Victoria. We embarked at the point Speke had identified in 1858 as the source of the Nile, and I took pictures very similar to ones I had taken in 1988.

We spent a while cruising near the shore, looking at kingfishers, cormorants, marabou storks, pelicans, vervet monkeys and monitor lizards. Afterwards across open water to a small island resort which we walked around. There were egrets aplenty, and we saw a monitor stealing egret eggs. A soda at the bar, back to Jinja and then to Entebbe for the flight home.

Thus ended the latest – and in all likelihood the last – of my African encounters.

CHAPTER 24

Retrospect

It is half-a-century since I first set foot in Africa. These fifty years have seen immense changes. When Africa has featured in the news in Europe it has been, with few exceptions, bad news. The principal exceptions have of course been the overthrow of white racism in southern Africa, with the end of Portuguese rule and of apartheid; and these did not herald the end of conflict or a dramatic transformation in the lives of the poor. Bad news told of droughts and famines; of inter-ethnic conflicts and civil wars; of vicious tyrants; of extensive corruption and massive indebtedness; of the deathly spread of AIDS; of failed states, terrorism and piracy; of venomous homophobia.

But there is a shinier side to the coin. A dramatic decline in under-five and maternal mortality (and if Africa still has the world's highest rates, that is because there has been round-the-globe improvement). A huge increase in the numbers with access to safe drinking water. Far more people at lower risk of malaria, thanks to impregnated mosquito nets. Tuberculosis, river blindness and trachoma still rife, but steadily decreasing. The number of children enrolled in primary education has soared. And, despite numerous and well-publicised exceptions, the poor are not as poor as they were fifty years ago and life expectancy has lengthened.

Furthermore, in the course of five decades Africa has seen a great increase in the number of Christian believers, of many persuasions, practices and theologies. They all appear to have in common their fervour, their confidence in the gospel, and the sheer joyfulness of their worship. I have heard plenty of moans from people with plenty to moan about, and yet my overwhelming experience is of a happy and generous people.

In 1987 I represented British Methodists at a consultation held by the World Council of Churches at El Escorial, near Madrid, on the subject of Resource-Sharing. It was still the case that North Atlantic Christians, with their rich material resources, had much to offer the Churches in the world's poorer regions. But Christianity was no longer a western religion; its demography had been transformed by the multiplication of believers in the south. There were rich spiritual resources that African, Asian, Pacific, Caribbean and Latin American Christians could share.

We discussed principles and methods, obstacles and opportunities; and because we were an international, culturally diverse gathering, we lived what we debated. Thus it was here that I was introduced to some of the African music that has subsequently enriched British worship, popularized by John Bell, Geoff Weaver and, among others, myself.

I do not have a cabinet-full of African curios. But forty years ago I brought back to England a handful of instruments. A roughly carved drum from Zambia. A calabash gourd hung with a net of cowrie shells (once the trading currency of much of west Africa), that is shaken rhythmically, either vigorously or softly. A small balafon, a kind of xylophone with wooden keys over resonators made of calabashes of different sizes.

Now the worse for wear, they remain – like the smell of some of my old books, and like my pre-digital photos – lasting mementos.

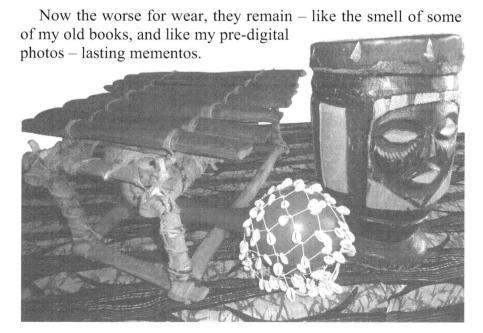

The drum and the cowrie-calabash have many times accompanied songs I first learned at El Escorial.

Of them all, my favourite is *Thuma Mina*. There are various renditions to be heard on YouTube. The Zulu words are translated, '*Send me Jesus, send me Jesus, send me Jesus, send me Lord.*'

I am for ever grateful that I was sent to Africa.